PENGUIN BOOKS

THE HAND GUIDE TO THE

BIRDS

OF NEW ZEALAND

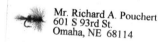

THE HAND GUIDE TO THE
BIRDS
OF NEW ZEALAND

Hugh A. Robertson
&
Barrie D. Heather

Illustrated by Derek J. Onley

PENGUIN BOOKS

To Lea & Rosemary

PENGUIN BOOKS

Penguin Books (NZ) Ltd, cnr Airborne and Rosedale Roads, Albany,
Auckland 1310, New Zealand
Penguin Books Ltd, 27 Wrights Lane, London W8 5TZ, England
Penguin USA, 375 Hudson Street, New York, NY 10014, United States
Penguin Books Australia Ltd, 487 Maroondah Highway, Ringwood, Australia 3134
Penguin Books Canada Ltd, 10 Alcorn Avenue, Toronto, Ontario, Canada M4V 3B2
Penguin Books (South Africa) Pty Ltd, 4 Pallinghurst Road, Parktown,
Johannesburg 2193, South Africa
Penguin Books India (P) Ltd, 11, Community Centre, Panchsheel Park,
New Delhi 110 017, India

Penguin Books Ltd, Registered Offices: Harmondsworth, Middlesex, England

First published by Penguin Books (NZ) Ltd, 1999

5 7 9 10 8 6 4

Copyright © text, Hugh A. Robertson and Barrie D. Heather 1999
Copyright © illustrations, Ornithological Society of New Zealand Inc. 1996

The right of Hugh A. Robertson and Barrie D. Heather to be identified as the authors of this work in terms of
section 96 of the Copyright Act 1994 is hereby asserted.

Designed by Richard King
Typeset by Egan-Reid Ltd, Auckland
Inside cover maps by Chris Edkins
Printed in Hong Kong

CONTENTS

INTRODUCTION

The *Hand Guide to the Birds of New Zealand* aims to help you to identify birds in New Zealand. On the page opposite the colour plate is a distribution map for those species breeding in New Zealand, and sufficient plumage and behavioural details that should help you to identify the species, sex and/or age of the bird you see in the field. For most landbirds breeding in New Zealand, there is no significant seasonal change in distribution as the equable climate of New Zealand means that there is no need for major migration, although there is some evidence of altitudinal migration and local movements to good food sources. The native cuckoos migrate to the tropical Pacific for our winter. Inland breeding waders, terns and gulls show the most obvious migration within New Zealand; Banded Dotterels, Gannets, White-fronted Terns and some seabirds visit Australia outside the breeding season, while many waders, terns and seabirds undertake major trans-equatorial migration, and some seabirds circle Antarctica between breeding seasons. Maps for vagrants, and for migratory waders (which can turn up in any estuary around the coast) are not necessary for identification purposes, and so this information is included in the text. The maps also show the distribution of birds on offshore islands in the New Zealand region, using initials in boxes to identify groups where the species is regularly found (starting in the top right and moving clockwise: K = Kermadecs, Ch = Chathams, Ant = Antarctica, Bo = Bounty Islands, An I = Antipodes, Ca = Campbell Islands, Ak = Auckland Islands, Sn = Snares). This book also includes a brief introduction to a dozen sites where a good range of native or endemic species should be found

— this is not a true locality guide, but may help overseas visitors and locals taking up bird-watching to visit a wide geographical range of the better birding sites in New Zealand, and at the same time see some of the country's most spectacular scenery.

For more detailed information about the ecology, behaviour and conservation of New Zealand birds we refer you to the parent publication of this book, *The Field Guide to the Birds of New Zealand* by Barrie Heather & Hugh Robertson published in New Zealand by Penguin, and offshore by Oxford University Press.

History

The Council of the Ornithological Society of New Zealand in 1959 asked Robert Falla, Dick Sibson and Graham Turbott to collaborate in compiling a practical field guide to the birds in the New Zealand region. The first edition, with 18 colour plates by Chloe Talbot Kelly, was published in 1966 and revised in 1970. In 1978, a further revision of the text was made and a new edition was published with 48 colour plates by Elaine Power. These various editions served as the 'bible' for several generations of bird-watchers in New Zealand, not only as a practical guide for identifying birds, but as a ready source of information on the distribution and habits of New Zealand birds. This tradition was continued in 1996 with the publication of *The Field Guide to the Birds of New Zealand*, which contained the 74 coloured plates by Derek Onley used in this book, and over 250 pages of text.

Derek Onley is a well-respected New Zealand ornithologist and wildlife artist. His 74 watercolour paintings depict all 328 species, and most subspecies, of birds officially recorded in the New Zealand region up to 1996. It is beyond the scope of this book to give all the information to allow identification to the subspecies level for all species, as this can often only be done with the bird in the hand.

Scope

For the purposes of this guide, the New Zealand region includes only New Zealand territory, from the Kermadec Islands at latitude 29°S to the Ross Dependency in Antarctica. We have included all species accepted on the New Zealand list from 1900 to 1996. We have therefore excluded records of vagrants recorded in the 1800s and of native birds that became extinct before 1900. We have included a specific plate that depicts those species that have probably become extinct during the 1900s in the slim hope that a few birds may survive somewhere; this plate also serves as a reminder of what we have recently lost from our New Zealand heritage.

The plates are arranged roughly in the standard taxonomic order, but where two similar-looking species are not closely related, they are shown together on the same plate. Two exceptions to this rule are a plate devoted to rare Australian vagrants, and the final plate which depicts the species that are probably extinct. The scientific world is in a state of transition between two different methods of ordering or listing the names of species. Scientific checklists and field guides have followed a consistent taxonomic ordering of species with groups that are thought to be closely related being placed alongside one another; however, new genetic techniques based on analysis of DNA and allozymes of different species indicate that we may soon have to completely rearrange the taxonomic ordering system. In the meantime, we have decided to follow the order and scientific names given in the *Checklist of the Birds of New Zealand*, with some very minor variations based on recently published work on the separation or amalgamation of subspecies.

Scientific names follow a standard format throughout the world and are traditionally given in italics with the genus listed first,

the species name second, and the subspecific name (if required) third. For example, the full scientific name for the Northern New Zealand Dotterel is *Charadrius obscurus aquilonius*. The word *Charadrius* refers to the genus, a group of related species (the Banded Dotterel and Black-fronted Dotterel also belong to this group of waders). The word *obscurus* distinguishes this particular species, and forms a unique combination with the word *Charadrius* to identify the species. Some species can be further divided into geographically distinct forms, called subspecies or races; these are distinguished by a third name; in this case *aquilonius* refers to the form breeding in the northern part of New Zealand, which are slightly different from those breeding on Stewart Island (*obscurus*). This subspecies is called the 'nominate' subspecies as it has the same subspecific name as the species name, which indicates that a bird of this form was first used to describe the species as being different from other dotterels.

We have also used the common names given in the *Checklist*, except that we have changed a few confusing prefixes, and have used our own personal preferences where a choice is available (e.g. Dunnock rather than the more confusing Hedgesparrow, given that they are not closely related to the 'true' sparrows). There is an international move to standardise the popular or common names of birds as well as the already accepted standardised scientific name. This move is prompted mainly by people who list all the species they have seen (variously known as listers, tickers or twitchers) who want to know if they can add a tick to their 'world list' if they see, for example, a 'Red-billed Gull' in New Zealand having seen a 'Silver Gull' in Australia — they can't because they belong to the same species. We have resisted attempts to internationalise the common names used in New Zealand because calling our Red-billed Gulls 'Silver Gulls' would add confusion because our endemic Black-billed Gull is more silver-coloured than the Red-billed Gull! Some species in New Zealand are known to everyone by their Maori name, e.g. Tui, Takahe, and we resist a loss of part of our heritage by imposing artificial labels on New Zealand birds. We have given the most widely accepted Maori name(s), but not all, as some species (e.g. Stitchbird) have up to seven recorded geographical variations of their Maori names. We have followed Maori usage by not adding 's' to plurals.

Instead of just giving body length from the tip of the bill to the tip of the tail, we have also tried to give an impression of the size of the bird by giving the weight. Where males and females differ appreciably in size, these are given separately. The weights are only approximate, as they are highly variable, depending on such things as time of year, the time of day, stage in the breeding cycle, and weights can be greatly inflated when a bird is preparing to lay, moult or migrate.

Acknowledgements

It would have been impossible to compile a book of this nature without considerable help from many others. We are extremely grateful for the time and efforts of the following people who have provided information on the top birding sites, checked our text, commented constructively on artwork, or allowed free access to museum collections:

Sandy Bartle, Kevin Bartram, Brian Bell, Peter Bull, Lindsay Charman, Les Cristidis, David Crouchley, Peter Dilks, Sue Ford, Brian Gill, Noel Hyde, Mike Imber, Bryan Jensen, Linda Lawrence, Rory O'Brien, Colin O'Donnell, Ralph Powlesland, Chris Robertson, Lea Robertson, Paul Sagar, Peter Schweigman, Graeme Taylor, Alan Tennyson, Geoff Tunnicliffe, Barbara Walters and Keith Woodley .

Chris Edkins drew the inside cover maps.

Ken Simpson, Ray Richards, David Medway, Geoff Walker and Richard King helped to get this book off the ground by helping with the concept and production of the parent publication. Nicola Strawbridge worked on the production of this hand guide.

To all, a big thank you!

Ornithological Society of New Zealand

The OSNZ has supported the production of this hand guide by commissioning Derek Onley to paint the 74 colour plates used earlier in *The Field Guide to the Birds of New Zealand*. Royalties on sales of this book will help the OSNZ to support more bird study within New Zealand. The object of the OSNZ, which was founded in 1939, is to encourage, organise and carry out ornithological field work on a national scale. No special qualifications are needed for membership, excepting an interest in the study of the habits and distribution of birds.

Because members are scattered throughout New Zealand and overseas, the Society operates chiefly by organising co-operative investigations, encouraging individual projects, and by issuing publications such as the quarterly scientific journal *Notornis* and accompanying newsletter, *OSNZ News*. An ornithological library containing many of the world's leading ornithological journals is maintained at the Auckland Institute and Museum. The main field activities include collection of nesting records and of data on storm-killed seabirds, special inquiries on the status of birds common and rare, and studies of the movements of birds throughout the country.

Further information about the OSNZ can be obtained from the Secretary, P.O. Box 12397, Wellington, New Zealand.

WHERE TO SEE BIRDS IN NEW ZEALAND

By international standards, New Zealand has a small number of species (the record seen in a day is about 75 species), but what it lacks in diversity, it makes up in uniqueness. The 12 sites listed here are not necessarily the best birding places in New Zealand, but they provide a wide geographical spread of good birding sites, often in spectacular or interesting settings. The sites are easily accessible, cover a range of habitat types, and should allow you to see or hear a good variety of native and endemic species during a visit. Many species (e.g. *Australasian Harrier*, *Pukeko*, *Variable Oystercatcher*, *NZ Pigeon* and *Fantail*) can be seen almost anywhere and so they are not included in the lists of notable native species you are likely to see at each site. Others are sufficiently rare that the chances of seeing them on a site visit are so low that it would be misleading to raise your hopes too much. Even if you manage to visit all 12 sites, many native species will still be missed, either because they have a limited distribution that doesn't include these sites, or because they were not apparent during your particular visit. The distribution and conspicuousness of birds can vary through the year and so you should bear this in mind when planning a visit to a particular site.

We have included information about sites that was accurate in 1999, but site conditions, operators, charges, contact information and schedules will change over time.

Aroha Island, Bay of Islands

This 12 ha 'island' in the Bay of Islands is owned by the Queen Elizabeth II National Trust and is the site of the Aroha Island Ecological Centre. The island is actually connected to the mainland by a causeway, and is situated about 10 km north-east of the Kerikeri Stone Store (one of the oldest buildings in New Zealand). Access is via Landing, Kapiro, Redcliffs, Rangitane and Kurapari Roads. The island is open to the general public 0930 to 1730 Tuesday to Sunday, except for July and August, with entry by donation; however, various forms of accommodation (self-catering cottage, bed & breakfast, and camping/campervan sites) are available on the island all year round. The Ecological Centre has good educational displays, including material on the star attraction of the site, the *Brown Kiwi*. An overnight stay is necessary to hear or possibly see them on the island; a two-hour guided night tour is available from the manager of the centre by arrangement @ $40 for 1-2 people. A wide range of bush, wetland and estuarine birds, are also seen here, including *Reef Heron, Banded Rail* and *Morepork*. Contact: Aroha Island Ecological Centre 09 407 5243, fax: 09 407 5246, e-mail: g.blunden@auckland.ac.nz

Tiritiri Matangi Island

This 220 ha island is an open sanctuary run by the Department of Conservation. It lies 3.5 km off the tip of the Whangaparaoa Peninsula and 25 km from downtown Auckland. The Department of Conservation and Supporters of Tiritiri Matangi Inc. are restoring the island from mainly farmland back to a forest haven for birds, and so apart from several valleys of mature forest, most vegetation is less than 20 years old. Because all mammalian predators have been eradicated, and many species re-introduced, the island has a particularly abundant and diverse birdlife. Gulf Harbour Ferries (09 424 5561, e-mail: wendy@gulfharbourferries.co.nz) depart Auckland and Gulf Harbour (near the tip of the Whangaparaoa Peninsula) on Thursdays,

Saturdays and Sundays (extra days in summer). Fuller's (09 367 9111) also run trips in the summer, and the Adventure Cruising Co. (09 444 9342, e-mail: adventure_cruise@clear.net.nz) call at the island during 3-day bird cruises between October and March. On the journey from Auckland you may see: *Flesh-footed Shearwater, Buller's Shearwater, Fluttering Shearwater, Common Diving Petrel, Australasian Gannet, Pied Shag* and *Arctic Skua*. The resident rangers will welcome you to the island and explain about its history and the restoration work; they will be able to advise you about the best birding sites on the island. A day visit should reveal *Blue Penguin* (in nesting and roosting boxes along the shore from the wharf), *Brown Teal, Takahe, Red-crowned Parakeet, Whitehead, NZ Robin, Tui, Bellbird, Stitchbird, Saddleback* and *Kokako*. *Spotless Crake* are heard occasionally in swampy areas, especially in Wattle Valley.

Miranda

The Firth of Thames, 50 km south-east of Auckland, is one of the best and most accessible wader sites in the country. The area is approached from Auckland by a scenic but winding route via Takanini or Papakura and Clevedon on the Blue Pacific Highway (watch for *Pied Shag* and *Spotted Shag* along the coast), or more directly from either north or south from SH2 or SH25. The major roosts are on the western coast between Kaiaua and Miranda, and these shellbanks and freshwater pools are easily accessible. The only bird observatory in New Zealand is situated 2 km north of Miranda and 6.5 km south of Kaiaua (famed for its excellent fish & chips) and is run by the Miranda Naturalists' Trust. The observatory (phone/fax 09 232 2781, e-mail: shorebird@xtra.co.nz) has comfortable accommodation and self-catering facilities at $15/person, or $45/couple for the use of a self-contained flat in the observatory. The resident manager can advise day visitors or overnight guests about the best places to see particular species, and a blackboard lists the species seen recently in the area. A high tide visit to Access Bay (just south of the observatory) at any time of year should reveal: *Pied Oyster-catcher, NZ Dotterel, Banded Dotterel, Wrybill* and *Black-billed Gull*, along with numerous Arctic waders from October to March, especially *Bar-tailed Godwit, Lesser Knot, Turnstone, Whimbrel, Red-necked Stint, Terek Sandpiper, Sharp-tailed Sandpiper, Curlew Sandpiper* and *Pacific Golden Plover*. Many Arctic migrants overwinter, but the diversity is usually not so great. In summer, a few *Eastern Curlew* roost near the old limeworks site near Miranda or on the shellbanks at Access Bay, and *Little Tern* are regular visitors to the area.

Rotorua

The Rotorua area is famed for its impressive geothermal attractions of geysers, boiling mud and hot pools, and it also has displays of Maori culture, New Zealand agriculture, and trout. *Brown Kiwi* are displayed in nocturnal houses at Rainbow & Fairy Springs and at the NZ Maori Arts & Crafts Institute. Lake Rotorua is host to a wide variety of waterfowl, and the best place to see them is at Sulphur Bay, a wildlife refuge, on the edge of downtown Rotorua. A walkway follows the shoreline from Rotorua City Lakefront Reserve east to Motutara Point and then along the western edge of Sulphur Bay to the Polynesian Spa. The peaceful Government Gardens and active thermal vents provide a unique backdrop to bird-watching. In spring and summer, *Pied Stilt, Spur-winged Plover, Banded Dotterel, Red-billed Gull* and *Black-billed Gull* nest on the silica flats in Sulphur Bay. *NZ Dabchick, Little Shag, Little Black Shag, Black Shag* and *NZ Scaup* nest in willows along the shoreline or on the island at Motutara Point. Other resident waterfowl include *Black Swan, Paradise Shelduck, Grey Duck, Grey Teal* and *Australasian Shoveler*.

Manawatu Estuary / Lake Horowhenua

A visit to the mouth of the Manawatu River at Foxton Beach provides a good opportunity to see a wide range of waders and other wetland birds. Turn west off SH1 at Foxton and a couple of kilometres into Foxton Beach township turn left at crossroads where the main road turns right. Follow signs to the motor camp and turn left into a track through tall trees as though to go to the motor camp, but then drive past the motor camp and park near the edge of the trees. The main high tide roost is on a sandspit extending eastward from the pines. Species likely to be seen at roost, or feeding on mudflats either side of high tide include *Pied Oystercatcher, Banded Dotterel, Wrybill* (January to July), and a variety of Arctic waders, especially *Bar-tailed Godwit, Lesser Knot, Pacific Golden Plover* and *Sharp-tailed Sandpiper*. A variety of terns often call in during the summer and autumn, and *Royal Spoonbill* often feed on the mudflats about 1 km upstream from the high tide roost. About 15 km to the south is Lake Horowhenua, a good site to see waterfowl. In Levin, turn west off SH1 into Queen Street West at the traffic lights opposite to where SH57 joins. Follow the road 2.5 km to the domain, where *NZ Dabchick, Australasian Shoveler, Grey Teal* and *Paradise Shelduck* are found around the northern shore of the lake. A few *Black-billed Gull* roost at the domain in winter.

Kapiti Island

This 1965 ha island is New Zealand's premier nature reserve as it has been cleared of all mammalian pests, and a large range of forest birds abound. It is run by the Department of Conservation and strict conditions apply to visitors to maintain the quality of the reserve. A maximum of 50 people are permitted to visit the island each day (no overnight stays), except Christmas Day, Boxing Day and New Years Day (permit fee: $8/adults and $4/children). Bookings are accepted up to 3 months in advance of the travel date, and it is recommended that you book early, especially for visits at the weekend or during the summer holidays. When you book, you will be advised how to contact the concessionaires who run the boat trips to the island from Paraparaumu Beach. The tariff is $30/person. Trips depart at 0900 and return at 1530 to 1600. Your bags will be inspected to ensure that you aren't accidentally carrying any rodents, and you will be given a short

talk about the island on your arrival. One-hour guided walks are available for $15/person, but visitors are allowed to wander the various tracks. Most birds can be seen within 500 m of the landing site at Rangatira Point, but many visitors still climb to the summit (521 m) where spectacular views of the Cook Strait region can be had on a fine day. It is recommended that people going to the summit climb the Trig Track and return down the more gently-graded Wilkinson Track. Birds likely to be seen during a day trip at any time of year include: *Fluttering Shearwater, Blue Penguin* (look in burrows with splashes of white guano at the entrance), *Paradise Shelduck, Weka, Takahe, Kaka, Red-crowned Parakeet, NZ Pipit, Whitehead, Tomtit, NZ Robin, Stitchbird, Bellbird, Tui, Kokako* (scarce) and *Saddleback. Arctic Skua* and *Long-tailed Cuckoo* could be added in the summer. Contact: Department of Conservation, P.O. Box 5086, Wellington, 04 472 7356, fax: 04 471 2075.

Kaikoura

This small seaside township lies about halfway between Picton and Christchurch, and is overlooked by the majestic Seaward Kaikoura Mountains, nesting site of the rare *Hutton's Shearwater*. A deep marine canyon lies just offshore and upwellings of cold nutrient-rich water make this a highly productive feeding ground for seabirds and marine mammals. Kaikoura is best known for its whale watching (mainly sperm whale) and opportunities to watch or swim with dusky dolphins and NZ fur seals. Weather permitting, OceanWings (03 319 6777, fax: 03 319 6534, e-mail: info@oceanwings.co.nz) run three specialist pelagic seabird cruises per day, each lasting 2-3 hours @ $60/adult or $35/child. These trips run all year, but May-September are the most productive months. The following species are regularly seen: *Wandering Albatross, Royal Albatross, Black-browed Mollymawk, Shy Mollymawk, Buller's Mollymawk, Flesh-footed Shearwater, Sooty Shearwater, Fluttering Shearwater, Hutton's Shearwater, Common Diving Petrel, Westland Petrel, White-chinned Petrel, Grey-faced Petrel, Cape Pigeon, Southern Giant Petrel, Northern*

Giant Petrel, Fairy Prion and *Grey-backed Storm Petrel*. On shore, the tip of the peninsula has huge colonies of *Red-billed Gull* and *White-fronted Tern*, and *Turnstone* and the occasional *Wandering Tattler* feed on the wave platforms amongst the NZ fur seals. A good range of accommodation is available in Kaikoura. Contact Kaikoura Information and Tourism (03 319 5641, fax: 03 319 6819, e-mail: info@kaikoura.co.nz), but the Kaikoura Youth Hostel (03 319 5931) and neighbouring Panorama Motel (03 319 5053, fax: 03 319 6605, e-mail: panorama.motel@xtra.co.nz) on The Esplanade both have stunning views across the sea to the mountains.

Arthur's Pass

This alpine pass is on the main road (SH73) and trans-alpine railway from Christchurch to the West Coast. A variety of accommodation is available in Arthur's Pass village. A stop at the Department of Conservation Visitor Centre is recommended to get advice about the various walks available in the National Park and around the village, and for the latest information on particular species. Approaching from Christchurch, look for *Australasian Crested Grebe* on Lake Pearson to the right of the main road about 25 km past Porters Pass (8 km before Cass) and *Black-fronted Tern* on the Waimakariri River. At night, *Great Spotted Kiwi* are often heard calling from the hills around the village, however, they are unlikely to be seen. Daytime bush walks should reveal *Rifleman, Brown Creeper, Tomtit, NZ Robin* and *Bellbird*. *Kea* are heard and occasionally seen around the village, but some usually hang out at the Otira Gorge lookout. *Blue Duck, Kaka* and *Tui* are best seen in the Otira Valley on the West Coast side of the pass. In summer and autumn, *Rock Wren* are sometimes seen above the bushline in Temple Basin, a 500 m (2 hour) climb through beech forest.

Eglinton Valley / Milford Sound

The very scenic drive from Te Anau to Milford Sound, via the Eglinton and upper Hollyford Valleys, passes through several very good bird-watching spots, which offer chances to see a wide range of native birds.

In summer, *Black-fronted Tern* nest on the Eglinton River. *Blue Duck* are sometimes seen in Monkey Creek, Falls Creek or the main Hollyford River and *NZ Scaup* are on most lakes. Bush birds include: *NZ Falcon, Kaka, Yellow-crowned Parakeet, Long-tailed Cuckoo, Rifleman, Yellowhead, Brown Creeper, Tomtit, NZ Robin, Bellbird* and *Tui*; the best places to stop to look for them are Smithy Creek, Lake Gunn nature walk, north of the Deer Flat camping area, and Lake Lochie near the 'Divide'. *Kea* are also found at the latter, around the Homer tunnel, and at 'The Chasm' on the Milford side. By following the Gertrude Saddle Track a short distance up the Gertrude Valley from the Homer Huts (1.5 km east of the Homer tunnel), you should come across *Rock Wren*; they are occasionally seen on the nature trail near the eastern portal to the Homer tunnel. At Milford Sound, cruise boats run 10 day trips (October-April) or 3 day trips (May-September) down the spectacular fiord to near the Tasman Sea, and some cruises stop at an underwater observatory in Harrison Cove where surprisingly colourful corals, sponges, anemones and fish can be viewed from 12 m under the surface. During the 2-3 hour ($42-50/adult, $10-16/child) round trip, *Fiordland Crested Penguin* are often seen on the northern shores of the fiord — contact: Milford Sound Red Boats Cruise (03 249 7926, fax: 03 249 8094, e-mail: redboats@milford.co.nz).

Otago Peninsula

Dunedin City and its environs are sometimes referred to as the 'Wildlife Capital of New Zealand' because of the wide range of wildlife and natural habitats within close reach of the city. The Otago Peninsula is the jewel in the crown of the area, and a number of ecotourism operators conduct general wildlife tours (contact Dunedin Visitor Information Centre 03 474 3300, fax: 03 474 3311). The Otago Peninsula Trust (03 478 0498, fax: 03 478 0575) operate a specialist observatory to view the unique *Northern Royal Albatross* colony at Taiaroa Head, where birds come and go all year round. Entry can be gained through one of the land-based tours or at the centre itself; however, in summer and at weekends bookings should be made in advance. Nearby, Southlight Wildlife (03 478 0287, fax: 03 478 0089) and Penguin Place (03 478 0286), both on Harington Point Road, offer good opportunities to get excellent views of *Yellow-eyed Penguin* and *Blue Penguin*. Monarch Wildlife Cruises (03 477 4276, fax: 03 477 4216) operate wildlife cruises from Dunedin City and Wellers Rock wharf, near Taiaroa Head, to give close views of the albatross colony, cliff-nesting *Spotted Shag* and *Stewart Island Shag*, penguins and other wildlife.

Stewart Island

The southernmost of the three main islands of New Zealand is reached by light aircraft (Southern Air Ltd, 03 218 9129, fax: 03 214 4681), or by fast ferry across Foveaux Strait from Bluff (Stewart Island Marine Ltd, 03 212 7660, fax: 03 212 8377). A wide range of seabirds can sometimes be seen on this crossing, but the ferries usually travel too fast for good bird-watching. Halfmoon Bay is a delightful fishing village of about 400 people, nestled into the bush surrounding Halfmoon and Horseshoe Bays. A wide variety of accommodation is available, ranging from backpackers to luxury lodges (contact the Stewart Island Visitor Centre, P.O. Box 3, Stewart Island, 03 219 1218, fax: 03 219 1555 or e-mail: stewartislandfc@doc.govt.nz for details). Bush birds such as *Weka*, *Kaka*, *Red-crowned Parakeet*, *Yellow-crowned Parakeet*, *Morepork*, *Brown Creeper*, *Tomtit*, *Bellbird* and *Tui* abound around the village or on nearby Ulva Island. From the tip of Akers Point (a 1 km walk from the village centre) a good range of seabirds can be seen, including *Black-browed Mollymawk*, *Shy Mollymawk*, *Southern Buller's Mollymawk*, *Sooty Shearwater*, *Common Diving Petrel*, *Cape Pigeon*, *Southern Giant Petrel*, *Northern Giant Petrel*, *Fairy Prion*, *Broad-billed Prion*, *Yellow-eyed Penguin*, *Blue Penguin*, *Spotted Shag* and *Stewart Island Shag*, and the occasional *Antarctic Tern*; however, a boat charter should give you a better chance to get amongst these seabirds and add to this list of species that abound around the Muttonbird Islands,

the mouth of Paterson Inlet and the east coast of the island. Bravo Adventure Cruises (phone/fax: 03 219 1144) run such cruises for $650/day or $450/half day, and also an excellent 4 hour evening visit for $60/person on alternate nights for moderately fit people to view free-living *Brown Kiwi* (Southern Tokoeka) feeding on invertebrates amongst the tidal wrack on a remote beach — flash photography is not permitted. A trip to Mason Bay via a water taxi to Freshwater Landing and a 4 hour (sometimes muddy) walk to Mason Bay Hut, and then a 20 minute walk to the beach down Duck Creek is a must for seabird enthusiasts. Seabirds are often wrecked on this wild, west-facing sandy beach, especially in the 3 km section south of Duck Creek. Species often found include albatrosses and mollymawks, *Sooty Shearwater*, *Common Diving Petrel*, *Fairy Prion*, *Broad-billed Prion*, *Mottled Petrel*, *Snares Crested Penguin* and *Fiordland Crested Penguin*. *Brown Kiwi* are often seen at night or even in daylight near Mason Bay hut and *NZ Dotterel* and other waders sometimes roost on sandflats 200 m due south of the first creek crossing below the hut. Charter aircraft from Southern Air Ltd or the Southland Aero Club (03 218 6171) can land on the beach at Mason Bay at low tide.

Chatham Island

This small cluster of islands, lying about 800 km east of Christchurch has many rare endemic birds, but some are inaccessible on small island nature reserves. Main Chatham Island, with a population of about 700 people is reached by 4 weekly flights from Wellington (3) or Christchurch (1) — contact Air Chathams (03 305 0209 or 04 388 9737). Visitors can hire vehicles from Chatham Motors (03 305 0093), and a range of accommodation is available: backpackers (03 305 0057), motel (03 305 0157), hotel (03 305 0048) and lodge (03 305 0196).

Weka and *NZ Pipit* abound throughout the island, and *Grey Duck* are moderately common. *Chatham Island Shag* and *Pitt Island Shag* are common around the coast and a mixed colony is found on cliffs at Matarakau

Point on the northern coast. *Chatham Island Oystercatcher* nest on many parts of the coast, especially on low rocky headlands and stream mouths on the northern coast, especially at Cape Pattison, Maunganui Beach and at Taupeka Point. *Banded Dotterel*, a variety of Arctic waders, and numerous *Black Swan* are found on the north-eastern shore of Te Whanga Lagoon between Hapupu and Ocean Mail. Forest birds such as *Chatham Island Pigeon, Red-crowned Parakeet* and *Chatham Island Warbler* are best seen at the Tuku Nature Reserve in the south-western corner of Chatham Island. Permission to cross private land must be obtained from Bruce and Liz Tuanui who live south of the Awatotara valley on the Tuku Road, and all gates on the road must be left as they are found. It is advisable to walk the last 2-3 km across the Tuku Valley to the bush around 'Taiko Town'. Follow the bush edge eastwards to get a view over the Tuku Valley from the spur where *Chatham Island Taiko* were dramatically rediscovered in 1978. Sea-watching, or better still a boat charter from Waitangi or Owenga to Pitt Strait, should offer views of some of the numerous species of seabird that breed in the group, especially *Northern Royal Albatross, Northern Buller's Mollymawk, Chatham Island Mollymawk, Sooty Shearwater, Common Diving Petrel, Northern Giant Petrel, Broad-billed Prion, Grey-backed Storm Petrel, White-faced Storm Petrel* and *Blue Penguin*. A visit close to the shore of South East (Rangatira) Island would permit views of *Chatham Island Oystercatcher, Shore Plover* and *Brown Skua* on the wave platforms, but landing is not permitted.

GLOSSARY

Australasia: the region including Australia, eastern Indonesia, New Guinea, the south-western Pacific and New Zealand

axillaries: feathers of the 'armpit' where the underwing joins the body

carpal bar: a dark band at the bend of the folded wing, particularly noticeable in some immature terns

caruncles: fleshy growths on the facial skin of some shags near the nostrils

cere: fleshy covering of the upper bill of certain birds, e.g. hawks, parrots, pigeons; often brightly coloured

coverts: feathers that cover the bases of the main wing feathers and tail feathers

culmen: the ridge along the whole length or top of the upper mandible

decurved: downward-curved bill, e.g. of curlews, ibises and honeyeaters

dimorphic: species with two forms, usually of plumage or size, e.g. raptors, Stitchbird

eclipse: dull plumage assumed by males of, especially, ducks after breeding; they become very like females and immatures

endangered: likely to become extinct if not managed carefully

endemic: natural breeding range is New Zealand and nowhere else, e.g. kiwi and Kakapo

front: the forehead between the base of upper bill and the crown, e.g. White-fronted Tern

frontal shield: horny shield on the forehead, taking the place of feathers

gape: fleshy skin at the sides of the base of the bill

gular sac or pouch: the elastic naked skin of the throat that can be filled with food (pelicans) or air (boobies)

immature: stage of plumage between the first moult and full breeding plumage (= subadult)

introduced: a bird brought to New Zealand by people, not by its own efforts

juvenile: birds in their first plumage after replacing natal down (US = juvenal)

lobes: folds of skin on the toes, extending out for swimming and closing when feet are drawn back, e.g. grebes and coot; the equivalent of webs in ducks

mantle: the upper back

migrant: a species that moves annually and seasonally between breeding and non-breeding areas, either within New Zealand, e.g. Wrybill, or to other countries, e.g. Turnstone

nape: the back of a bird's neck

native: birds that are naturally found in New Zealand, e.g. Tui, including recently self-introduced species, e.g. the Spur-winged Plover from Australia

pelagic: of the ocean; feeding far out to sea

phase: different colour form within a species not related to age, sex or season, e.g. Little Shag

primaries: the outermost flight feathers

scapulars: feathers that lie along the upper shoulder of the wing, sometimes distinctively coloured, e.g. Black-fronted Dotterel

secondaries: flight feathers along the middle and inner portion of the wing

species: kinds of birds that may live together in the wild without normally interbreeding

speculum: iridescent patch on the secondaries of ducks; of different colour and on the upperwing only

straggler: a bird that follows its normal migratory path but goes too far or strays off course

subspecies: a geographical race of a species that has some slight, but consistent, differences from others of the species

tertials: small patch of generally longer flight feathers close to the base of the wing

threatened: species that are in low numbers or declining in number and/or range and which require management or intervention to ensure their survival

undulating: flight that dips up and down, e.g. some finches

vagrant: a wanderer; a bird having turned up unexpectedly in an unusual direction, having strayed there by mistake or having been caught up in a severe storm is blown well off course, whereas a straggler is in about the right direction but has gone further than usual

wattles: colourful fleshy drupes on either side of the gape in Saddleback, Kokako and Huia

wingbar: a band of contrast, usually white, on the upperwing in flight, often formed by the coloured tips of the wing-coverts

STANDARD REFERENCES

The following books provide information on the birds that are found in the New Zealand region. They have been the source of much information used to compile this hand guide and all are recommended for any private or public library collection.

Bull, P.C., Gaze, P.D. & Robertson, C.J.R. 1985. *The Atlas of Bird Distribution in New Zealand.* Wellington: Ornithological Society of New Zealand.

Chambers, S. 1989. *Birds of New Zealand: locality guide.* Hamilton: Arun Books.

Dunn, J.L. & Blom, E.A.T. 1992. *Field Guide to the Birds of North America.* Washington: National Geographic.

Harrison, P. 1988. *Seabirds: an identification guide.* London: Christopher Helm.

Hayman, P., Marchant, J. & Prater, T. 1986. *Shorebirds: an identification guide to the waders of the world.* Beckenham: Croom Helm.

Heather, B.D. & Robertson, H.A. 1996. *The Field Guide to the Birds of New Zealand.* Auckland: Viking.

Higgins, P.J. 1999. *Handbook of Australian, New Zealand and Antarctic Birds.* Vol. 4. Melbourne: Oxford University Press.

Higgins, P.J. & Davies, S.J.J.F. 1996. *Handbook of Australian, New Zealand and Antarctic Birds.* Vol. 3. Melbourne: Oxford University Press.

Jonsson, L. 1992. *Birds of Europe with North Africa and the Middle East.* London: Christopher Helm.

Maclean, G.L. 1993. *Roberts' Birds of Southern Africa.* London: New Holland.

Marchant, S. & Higgins, P. (eds). 1990. *Handbook of Australian, New Zealand and Antarctic Birds.* Vol. 1. Melbourne: Oxford University Press.

Marchant, S. & Higgins, P. (eds). 1993. *Handbook of Australian, New Zealand and Antarctic Birds.* Vol. 2. Melbourne: Oxford University Press.

Pizzey, G. 1980. *A Field Guide to the Birds of Australia.* Sydney: Collins.

Pratt, H.D., Bruner, P.L. & Berrett, D.G. 1987. *A Field Guide to the Birds of Hawaii and the Tropical Pacific.* Princeton: Princeton University Press.

Robertson, C.J.R. (ed.) 1985. *Reader's Digest Complete Book of New Zealand Birds.* Sydney: Reader's Digest.

Simpson, K. & Day, N. 1993. *Field Guide to the Birds of Australia.* Ringwood: Viking O'Neil.

Sinclair, I., Hockey, P. & Tarboton, W. 1993. *Illustrated Guide to the Birds of Southern Africa.* London: New Holland.

Turbott, E.G. 1990. *The Checklist of the Birds of New Zealand and the Ross Dependency, Antarctica.* Auckland: Random Century.

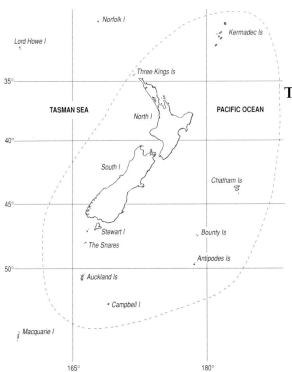

The New Zealand region

Norfolk I

Kermadec Is

Lord Howe I

Three Kings Is

35°

TASMAN SEA

PACIFIC OCEAN

North I

40°

South I

Chatham Is

45°

Stewart I

Bounty Is

The Snares

Antipodes Is

50°

Auckland Is

Campbell I

Macquarie I

165°

180°

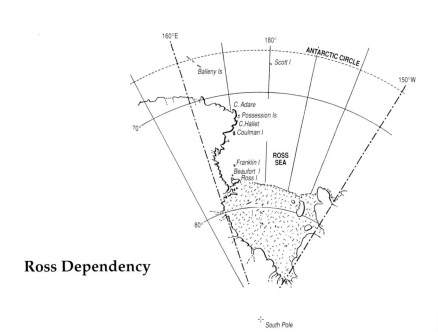

160°E

180°

ANTARCTIC CIRCLE

Balleny Is

Scott I

150°W

C. Adare

70°

Possession Is

C. Hallet

Coulman I

ROSS
SEA

Franklin I

Beaufort I

Ross I

80°

Ross Dependency

South Pole

Parts of a bird

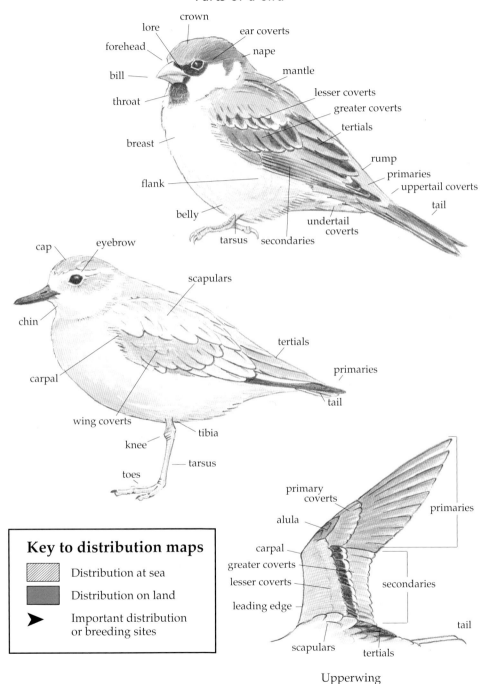

crown
lore
forehead
bill
throat
ear coverts
nape
mantle
lesser coverts
greater coverts
tertials
rump
primaries
uppertail coverts
tail
breast
flank
belly
tarsus
secondaries
undertail coverts

cap
eyebrow
scapulars
chin
tertials
primaries
carpal
wing coverts
knee
tibia
tarsus
toes
tail

primary coverts
alula
carpal
greater coverts
lesser coverts
leading edge
scapulars
tertials
primaries
secondaries
tail

Upperwing

Key to distribution maps

Distribution at sea

Distribution on land

Important distribution or breeding sites

Plate 1   **KIWI**

Small group of distinctive flightless and generally nocturnal birds. More often heard than seen; most vocal in the first two hours of darkness. Males smaller and have loud shrill clear ascending whistle; females deeper hoarse whistle, often given in response to male call; calls repeated 10–25 times. Large cone-shaped birds with small head and long bill with nostrils near tip; minute remnant wings and no tail; coarse loose feathers; strong legs and toes with long claws. Slow lumbering gait, but can run fast. In native forests, scrub, rough tussock grassland and in some exotic forests; from sea level to subalpine. Kiwi snuffle as they explore for food on ground. Feed on invertebrates (especially worms, bugs, beetles and spiders) and fallen fruits, from surface and by probing up to 10 cm into soil. Lay 1–2 huge white eggs in a burrow, hollow log or under dense vegetation. Very long incubation – by the male only in Little Spotted Kiwi and Brown Kiwi in the North Island, but by male and female in Great Spotted Kiwi and Brown Kiwi in the South Island, and by the pair plus helpers in Brown Kiwi on Stewart Island. Chicks hatch fully feathered, like miniature adults, and are mobile within a week but return to the nest each day for several weeks or even months.

BROWN KIWI (Tokoeka – South and Stewart Islands)   *Apteryx australis*
Uncommon endemic

40 cm; ♂ 2.2 kg, ♀ 2.8 kg. Dark greyish brown *streaked lengthways* reddish brown; *long* ivory bill. Male has shrill clear (or slightly warbling) ascending and then descending whistle; female has lower-pitched, hoarse cry. **Habitat:** Native forest, scrub, exotic forest (especially in Northland, Coromandel and Taranaki), rough farmland and tussockland (subalpine and dunes). Most common in Northland and on Stewart Island; small distinctive populations at Okarito (60–100 birds) and near Haast (200–300 birds). **Breeding:** Jun–Mar.

GREAT SPOTTED KIWI (Roa)   *Apteryx haastii*
Uncommon endemic

45 cm; ♂ 2.4 kg, ♀ 3.3 kg. Largest kiwi. Light brownish grey tinged with chestnut, mottled or banded *horizontally* with white; massive ivory bill; legs dark brown; claws vary from horn to black. Juvenile has proportionately longer bill and darker legs than similar Little Spotted Kiwi. Male very loud shrill warbling whistle; female slower and lower-pitched ascending warble; calls more powerful and slower than Little Spotted Kiwi. **Habitat:** Native forest, scrub, pakihi wetlands and tussock grassland from sea level to subalpine, but distribution patchy. Strongholds in north-western Nelson, Paparoa Ranges and between Lake Sumner and Arthur's Pass. **Breeding:** Jul–Dec.

LITTLE SPOTTED KIWI (Kiwi-pukupuku)   *Apteryx owenii*
Rare endemic

30 cm; ♂ 1150 g, ♀ 1325 g. Smallest kiwi. Brownish grey finely mottled or banded *horizontally* with white; long ivory bill; pale legs and claws. Male high-pitched ascending whistle; female lower and more tremulous; call rate faster and higher pitched than other kiwi, especially the female. **Habitat:** Native forest, scrub and grassland on a few offshore islands: c. 1,000 on Kapiti I, small populations have been established on Hen, Tiritiri Matangi, Red Mercury and Long (Marlborough) Is. Some may persist in Westland or Fiordland. **Breeding:** Sep–Feb.

BROWN KIWI

GREAT SPOTTED KIWI

LITTLE SPOTTED KIWI

Plate 2   **GREBES**

Freshwater diving birds with a distinctive silhouette – dumpy body, low to the water, with rounded rear end because of no visible tail; bill pointed; head held erect. Sexes alike. They feed underwater, propelled by special lobed feet. As their legs are set well back, they are awkward on land and seldom venture onto it. Patter across the water when disturbed or during displays, but can fly well at night. Gather in loose flocks in autumn and winter. Silent. Nests are bulky floating structures, often attached to emergent or overhanging vegetation. Lay 2–4 chalky white eggs, staining to brown; covered whenever the adult leaves the nest. Chicks are carried on an adult's back when very small. Young have striped heads, through to the age of independence.

AUSTRALASIAN CRESTED GREBE (Puteketeke)   *Podiceps cristatus*
Uncommon native

50 cm, 1100 g. A large long-necked grebe with a dagger-like bill and a prominent double crest and ruff. Swims with its slender white neck held erect, head horizontal. Brilliant white foreneck and chest visible when head lowered at rest. Adult plumage similar all year. Juveniles retain stripes on head until independent. Immature lacks ruff and has only a small crest, making it look like an immature Pied Shag. In flight, long thin body and prominent white panels on front and back of dark upperwing. Dives smoothly without splash. **Habitat:** Large open lakes of inland South I. Usually in pairs but gather on some Canterbury lakes in winter. A rare vagrant to North I. **Breeding:** Sep–Feb.

NEW ZEALAND DABCHICK (Weweia)   *Poliocephalus rufopectus*
Uncommon endemic

29 cm, 250 g. A small dark grebe with a dumpy body, slim neck, small head, short bill and tiny, fluffy white tail. *Blackish head, finely streaked with silver feathers; prominent yellow eye; rusty chestnut foreneck and breast.* After breeding, plumage paler and nondescript. After several months, juveniles look like adults. Dives frequently, often smoothly but sometimes after a leap. When alarmed, swims quietly away on or under the water, or skitters across the water, its rapidly beating wings hitting the surface. **Habitat:** Sheltered parts of lakes, farm ponds and, in winter, sewage oxidation ponds. Locally common in North I; a rare vagrant to South I. **Breeding:** Jun–Mar.

HOARY-HEADED GREBE   *Poliocephalus poliocephalus*   **Rare Australian vagrant**

28 cm, 250 g. Similar to NZ Dabchick in size and habits; *much paler and slimmer* than other small grebes. Breeding adult dark grey above, breast pale buff, *head prominently streaked silver* (hoary), eye not contrasting; bill tipped white. Non-breeding adult *pale grey with contrasting grey-brown cap to below eye* and extending as a dark stripe from the crown down the hindneck; bill pinkish. Regularly swims with thin neck held erect. **Habitat:** Lakes and farm ponds.

AUSTRALASIAN LITTLE GREBE   *Tachybaptus novaehollandiae*   **Rare native**

25 cm, 220 g. The smallest grebe in NZ. Breeding adult has black head with contrasting yellow eye, *a yellow patch of skin between eye and bill*, and broad band of rich chestnut on sides of neck. Non-breeding adult and immature lack head and neck colours, the skin patch becomes whitish and hard to see, but upperparts remain dark brown; *pale cheeks and foreneck contrast with dark brown cap to level of eye.* Dives frequently. Wary; when disturbed, dives and may lurk in vegetation, often with only its head above water. **Habitat:** Lakes and farm ponds.

AUSTRALASIAN CRESTED GREBE

juv

NEW ZEALAND DABCHICK

imm/non-breeding

HOARY-HEADED GREBE

breeding

non-breeding

AUSTRALASIAN LITTLE GREBE

breeding

non-breeding

Huge ('albatrosses') or very large ('mollymawks') seabirds with long narrow wings and short tail. Long heavy hooked bill covered with horny plates, nostrils in small tubes on the sides near the base. Most are dark above and mainly white below. Pattern of upperwing, underwing, head and bill are distinctive. In flight, soar gracefully on stiffly held wings, and only rarely flap. Clumsy on ground; legs and webbed feet set well back. Generally oceanic; occasionally seen near land. Many follow ships or gather around fishing boats. Silent at sea except when fighting over food. Loud bleats, croaks, whines and cackles at breeding colonies, and elaborate displays accompanied by bill-clapping and calls. Lay 1 large white egg in shallow bowl or on top of pedestal constructed of vegetation and mud. Long incubation period and extremely long fledging period (7–11 months for full breeding cycle). Sexes alike but males larger. Juveniles generally distinctive for several years.

ROYAL ALBATROSS (Toroa)   *Diomedea epomophora*   Locally common endemic

115 cm, 9 kg. Two races distinguished by size and amount of black on upperwings. Like the palest adult Wandering Albatrosses but with no distinctive juvenile plumage, wings normally black above or with white on the leading edge of the inner upperwing, and tail usually white; bill massive (170 x 65 mm), light pink with creamy tip and *with black cutting edge to upper mandible.* Juvenile has white body except for heavy black flecking on the back, flanks, crown and tail; upperwings black (Northern race *sanfordi*) or mainly black with small patches of white at base of leading edge and in centre of inner wing, becoming increasingly white from the leading edge backwards (Southern race *epomophora*). Adult has completely white body; upperwings black (Northern race) or black with white patches extending backwards from leading edge (Southern race); underwings white with black tip and thin black trailing edge. Legs and feet pinkish to bluish white. **Habitat:** Northern race breeds at Taiaroa Head (Dunedin) and Sisters and Forty Fours Is (Chathams); Southern race breeds Campbell and Auckland Is. Ranges widely circumpolar through the southern oceans, and most often seen in NZ coastal waters in winter, except off Taiaroa Head. **Breeding:** All year; eggs laid Oct–Dec; young fledge c. 11 months later.

WANDERING ALBATROSS   *Diomedea exulans*   Uncommon native

115 cm, 6.5 kg. Variable plumages, according to age and race. Some pale adults are like Royal Albatross, but all have a huge bill (160 x 55 mm), light pink with creamy tip and with *no black on cutting edges*; leading edge of inner upperwing usually black or mottled black in all but the whitest birds (which have much more extensive white on upperwings than the whitest Royal); tail usually black-tipped. Juvenile initially *uniformly dark brown, except for white face and dark-tipped white underwings* (A). Over the next 10–15 years, the plumage whitens, initially on the belly (B), then from the back onto the upperwings, and outwards from a central patch on the upperwing, following the progression from C to F in the whitest NZ breeding birds; however, birds breed in the NZ region in all forms from C through to F. Those birds in phase G, with white leading edge to upperwing, are of the larger race *chionoptera* (Snowy Albatross), which breeds outside the NZ region. Underwings white with black tip and thin black trailing edge. Legs and feet pinkish to brownish grey. **Habitat:** Breeds circumpolar subantarctic; in NZ region, breeds at Antipodes, Campbell and Auckland Is. Ranges widely through the southern oceans and most often seen in NZ coastal waters in winter. **Breeding:** All year; eggs laid Jan–Mar, young fledge c. 11 months later.

Southern

Northern

juv Northern

ROYAL
ALBATROSS

A
juv

B

WANDERING
ALBATROSS

C

D

E

F

G

Plate 4

ALBATROSSES

SHY MOLLYMAWK *Diomedea cauta*

Common native

90 cm, 4 kg. Three subspecies breed in NZ region, separated by size, plumage and bill colours. All have diagnostic *white underwing with very narrow black borders and a small black triangular notch at base of the leading edge*. Larger and longer-winged than other mollymawks. Adult NZ White-capped Mollymawk (*steadi*) has white head and neck, small black patch from eye to bill shading to very faint grey wash on cheeks; mantle grey-brown merging into grey-black back and upperwings; rump white, tail grey-black, underparts white; *tips of underwing white with thin black edging*: bill (133 mm) pale bluish horn with yellowish top to bill, especially at base and tip; legs and feet pale blue-grey. Salvin's Mollymawk (*salvini*) smaller; crown pale grey, more extensive light grey on face, throat, hindneck and mantle; *tips of underwing black*; sides of bill (128 mm) grey-green, with paler top and bottom, and dark spot at tip of lower bill. Chatham I Mollymawk (*eremita*) is smallest and darkest race; crown pale grey; face, throat, hindneck and mantle dark grey; tips of underwings black; bill (120 mm) *yellow with dark spot at tip of lower mandible*. Immatures of all subspecies have more extensive grey areas; underwing patterns are similar to that in adults; *bill bluish grey with black tips to both mandibles*. **Habitat:** Breeds subantarctic, mainly in NZ region; at Auckland and Antipodes Is (*steadi*), Bounty Is and The Snares (*salvini*), Pyramid Rock, Chathams (*eremita*). Races *steadi* and *salvini* range widely through southern oceans and often to NZ coastal waters, especially around boats; *eremita* is rarely seen away from Chathams but reported off eastern S America and sometimes beach-wrecked on NZ mainland. **Breeding:** Nov–Aug (*steadi*), Sep–Apr (*salvini* and *eremita*).

YELLOW-NOSED MOLLYMAWK *Diomedea chlororhynchos*

Uncommon visitor

75 cm, 2.5 kg. Small slender mollymawk. Adult has white head with small dark eye patch, sometimes with grey cheeks; neck, underparts and rump white; back, upperwings and tail black; underwings white with black tips and thin clear-cut black margins, wider on leading than trailing edge. *Bill slender (117 mm), black with yellow ridge deepening to reddish orange at the tip*. Immature similar but eye patch smaller; hindneck is washed grey; leading margin of underwing is broader and less clear-cut; *bill completely black*. **Habitat:** Breeds on islands in South Atlantic and South Indian Oceans. Ranges widely through warm subantarctic and subtropical waters, and a few regularly reach the Tasman Sea, Hauraki Gulf and Bay of Plenty, mostly in winter.

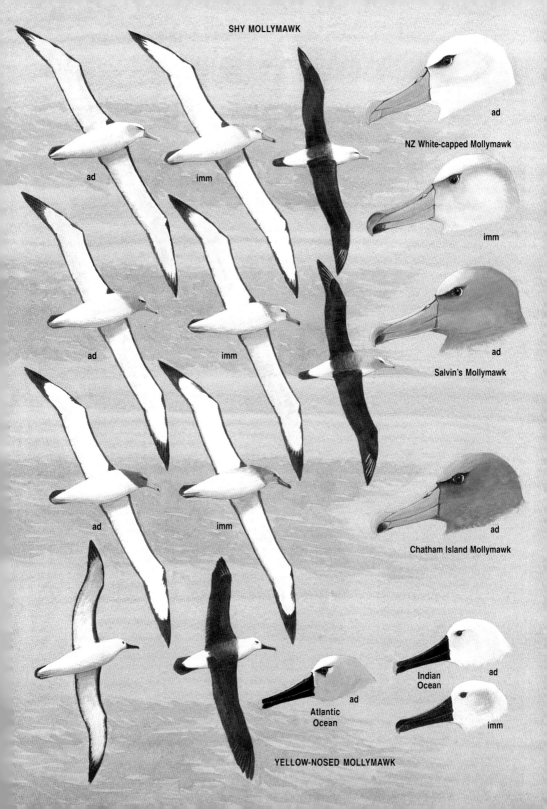

SHY MOLLYMAWK

ad

imm

ad

imm

ad

imm

ad

imm

ad

NZ White-capped Mollymawk

imm

ad

Salvin's Mollymawk

ad

Chatham Island Mollymawk

ad

imm

Indian
Ocean

ad

imm

ad

Atlantic
Ocean

YELLOW-NOSED MOLLYMAWK

Plate 5   **ALBATROSSES**

BLACK-BROWED MOLLYMAWK   *Diomedea melanophrys*   **Common native**

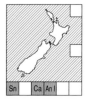

90 cm, 3 kg. Two subspecies in NZ region, separated by size, plumage and eye colour. Adult NZ Black-browed Mollymawk (*impavida*) has *whole body white except for heavy black triangle around eye* giving frowning appearance, blackish-grey back connecting black upperwings, and dark grey tail; underwings white with *broad black edges*, wider on the leading edge especially on the inner part of the wing; some have extensive dark streaking in armpits, almost connecting front to back; bill (110 mm) yellow with orange tip; *eye honey-coloured*; legs and feet pale bluish white. Subantarctic Black-browed Mollymawk (*melanophrys*) similar, but eyebrow smaller; underwings have less extensive, although still broad, black edges; bill (118 mm) heavier; *eye dark brown*. Immature NZ Black-browed Mollymawk like adult except eyebrow smaller; greyish wash on crown and hindneck; *underwings almost completely black*; bill greyish green with dark tip, turning yellow with a dark tip in older birds; eye white. Immature Subantarctic Black-browed Mollymawk similar, but eyebrow smaller; grey wash extends as a collar onto chest; eye dark brown. **Habitat:** NZ Black-browed Mollymawk breeds only at Campbell I; Subantarctic Black-browed Mollymawk breeds circumpolar subantarctic, including Bollons I (Antipodes), Western Chain (The Snares) and Campbell I. Ranges widely through southern oceans and into subtropical waters. Often seen off NZ coast or behind boats, especially in winter. **Breeding:** Sep–Apr.

GREY-HEADED MOLLYMAWK   *Diomedea chrysostoma*   **Locally common native**

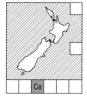

80 cm, 3.25 kg. Adult has *light grey head, throat, neck and mantle*, paler on forehead; dark grey patch around and ahead of eye, small but prominent white mark just behind eye; sharp margin on chest to white underparts, white rump, grey tail. Upperwings and back dark grey; underwings *white with broad black leading edge and narrow black trailing edge. Bill (113 mm) black with rich yellow along ridge and along bottom edge*, shading to rosy pink at tip; legs and feet greyish white. Immature similar, but initial darker grey on head wears to very pale on forehead and cheeks in some birds; underwings black or with narrow greyish or white central stripe. Bill dark grey, darker tip changing to dull yellow with age. **Habitat:** Breeds circumpolar subantarctic; in NZ region, only at Campbell I. Ranges widely through southern oceans, and a few visit NZ coastal waters, especially in winter. **Breeding:** Sep–May.

BULLER'S MOLLYMAWK   *Diomedea bulleri*   **Common endemic**

80 cm, 3 kg. Two subspecies in NZ region, separated by bill size and head plumage. Adult Southern Buller's Mollymawk (*bulleri*) has *silvery-white forehead*, contrasting light grey crown, black patch around and ahead of eye, small white crescent behind to below eye; neck, hindneck and throat grey, with sharp margin on chest from white underparts; rump white, tail grey. Upperwings and back dark grey; underwings *white with clear-cut broad black leading edge and very narrow black trailing edge*. Bill (118 x 27 mm) black with golden yellow along ridge and tip and along bottom edge; legs and feet pale bluish grey to grey-mauve. Northern Buller's Mollymawk (*platei*) similar but *forehead silvery grey*; darker grey on head and throat. Bill more robust (120 x 31 mm); feet darker. Immature like adult except whole head dark grey and bill brownish horn with darker tip. **Habitat:** Southern Buller's breeds The Snares and Solander Is; Northern Buller's breeds Three Kings and Chatham Is. Commonly seen off NZ coast or behind boats and trawlers offshore during breeding. An unknown proportion of the population disperses to eastern Pacific after breeding. **Breeding:** Jan–Oct (Southern), Oct–Jun (Northern).

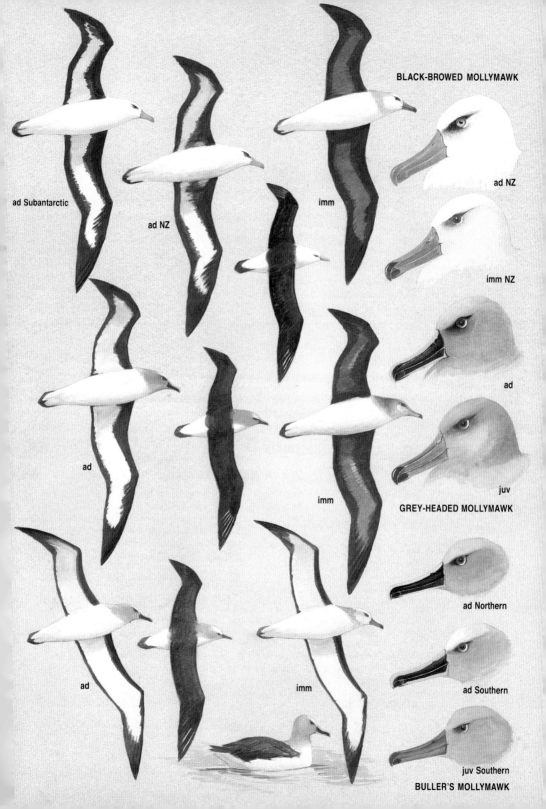

BLACK-BROWED MOLLYMAWK

ad Subantarctic

ad NZ

imm

ad NZ

imm NZ

ad

imm

ad

juv

GREY-HEADED MOLLYMAWK

ad Northern

ad

imm

ad Southern

juv Southern

BULLER'S MOLLYMAWK

Plate 6

SOOTY ALBATROSSES
and GIANT PETRELS

Sooty albatrosses are slender sooty brown and grey birds with black bill, long narrow wings and very long pointed tail.

LIGHT-MANTLED SOOTY ALBATROSS *Phoebetria palpebrata* Uncommon native

80 cm, 2.75 kg. Adult has sooty-brown head, throat and wings; *ash-grey back from nape to rump*, pale brownish-grey underparts. Bill (105 mm) slender, black with blue line along lower bill; legs and feet pale grey-flesh. Juvenile similar, but brown scalloping on neck and upper back, grey eye-ring and greyish-yellow line along lower bill. **Habitat:** Breeds circumpolar subantarctic; in NZ region, at Antipodes, Auckland and Campbell Is. Ranges widely at sea, and a few reach NZ waters or are beachwrecked, mainly in winter. **Breeding:** Oct–May.

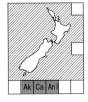

SOOTY ALBATROSS *Phoebetria fusca*   Rare vagrant

80 cm, 2.5 kg. Adult is entirely sooty brown except slightly darker on head and wings, white eye-ring, and pale shafts to primaries and tail. Bill (112 mm) slender, black with yellow line along lower bill; legs and feet pale grey-flesh. Juvenile similar but buff scalloping on collar and sides of neck; ash-grey nape, grey eye-ring and grey line along lower bill. **Habitat:** Breeds subantarctic and subtropical Atlantic and Indian Oceans. Recorded a few times in NZ waters.

The two giant petrels are very similar robust brown-to-white (rare) fulmarine petrels with short wings and tail. Massive pale bill with prominent nasal tubes. Flight laboured with burst of flapping interspersed with long glides and wheeling, not soaring. On land, mobile and can stand upright. Oceanic and coastal. Frequently follow ships and trawlers. Silent at sea except when fighting for food. Loud calls at colonies. Lay 1 large white egg in low cup-shaped bowl. Long incubation and fledging periods. Sexes alike but male larger; juveniles darker.

NORTHERN GIANT PETREL (Nelly) *Macronectes halli*   Common native

90 cm, 4.5 kg. Similar to dark phase Southern Giant Petrel, but *bill pinkish-yellow horn tipped brownish*, and face darker. Adult has greyish-brown body with paler forehead, sides of face and chin, sometimes white on chin and around base of bill. Bill robust (90–105 mm); eye grey to off-white. No white phase. Juvenile all dark sooty brown, fading to grey-brown with age; eye usually grey. **Habitat:** Breeds circumpolar subantarctic; in NZ region, at Chathams, Port Pegasus (Stewart I), Antipodes, Auckland and Campbell Is. Ranges widely through southern oceans and often seen in NZ waters, especially Cook Strait. **Breeding:** Aug–Feb.

SOUTHERN GIANT PETREL (Nelly) *Macronectes giganteus*   Common visitor

90 cm, 4.5 kg. Variable plumages; dark adults and juveniles are almost identical to Northern Giant Petrel except *bill yellowish horn, tipped green*, and face paler. Adult (dark phase) has white head, flecked brown, merging into greyish-brown body, wings and tail; often shows thin white leading edge to innerwings. Bill robust (90–105 mm); eye brown to grey, usually brown. Juvenile all dark sooty brown, fading to grey-brown with age; eye generally brown. Adult and juvenile (white phase) completely white except for scattered flecks of brown. **Habitat:** Breeds circumpolar subantarctic and around Antarctic coast; in NZ region, recorded breeding once at Cape Crozier, Antarctica. Ranges widely through southern oceans, and juveniles common in NZ waters, especially in winter and spring; a few adults reach NZ. **Breeding:** Sep–Apr.

LIGHT-MANTLED
SOOTY ALBATROSS

imm

SOOTY ALBATROSS

worn
plumage

juv

NORTHERN
GIANT PETREL

SOUTHERN
GIANT PETREL

juv

Plate 7

SHEARWATERS

Medium to large seabirds with long slender bill and nostrils encased in a short flattened tube. Sexes and ages alike; most are dark above and mainly white below, but some are all dark. Many species form large feeding flocks. Usually fly close to the surface, often with a series of rapid wingbeats followed by a glide, but in windy conditions can wheel high on stiffly held wings. Clumsy on ground; legs and webbed feet set well back. Range from coastal to oceanic. Some species are highly migratory. Most species very vocal at breeding colonies at night. Lay 1 large white egg, usually deep in a burrow. Long incubation and fledging periods.

BULLER'S SHEARWATER   *Puffinus bulleri*   Common endemic

46 cm, 425 g. Head and hindneck blackish brown; *back and upperwings frosty grey with bold dark M across wings, lower back and rump*; uppertail light grey with broad black tip to long wedge-shaped tail; sharp line of demarcation from white underparts and underwing. Bill long and slender (41 x 12 mm), bluish grey with darker tip; legs and feet pink with dark outer toes and outer edge of tarsus. **Habitat:** Breeds only at Poor Knights Is. Ranges widely around NZ coast and migrates to northern and eastern Pacific. **Breeding:** Nov–May.

WEDGE-TAILED SHEARWATER   *Puffinus pacificus*   Locally common native

46 cm, 450 g. Variable plumages but always with *broad wings and long wedge-shaped tail*. Rare pale phase has head, hindneck and upperparts dark brown with a sharp line of demarcation from white chin and throat; underparts mainly white but variably mottled brown on sides of breast, flanks and undertail; underwing white with dark borders and tip, mottled brownish grey on underwing coverts. Bill compressed (38 x 13 mm), slate grey; legs and feet pale flesh. See Plate 8 for dark phase. **Habitat:** Subtropical and tropical Pacific and Indian Oceans. Breeds on Kermadec Is and rarely reaches NZ mainland. **Breeding:** Dec–Jun.

Grey Petrel (see Plate 10)

PINK-FOOTED SHEARWATER   *Puffinus creatopus*   Rare subtropical vagrant

48 cm, 900 g. Head, hindneck and upperparts greyish brown; chin, throat and underparts mainly white, but some have greyish brown on chin, throat and flanks; underwings whitish with varying grey and white mottling. Bill heavy (42 mm), pinkish with a dark tip; legs and feet pink. **Habitat:** Breeds off Chile. Migrates to eastern N Pacific. A few have reached NZ waters, off east coast South I.

CORY'S SHEARWATER   *Calonectris diomedea*   Rare Atlantic vagrant

46 cm, 900 g. Head, hindneck and upperparts greyish brown; chin, throat and underparts white, without clear line of demarcation. *Underwing white*, with narrow dark margins and tips. *Bill large (57 x 21 mm), dull yellow with darker tip*; legs and feet fleshy pink, stained brown on outer toe and outer surface of tarsus. **Habitat**: Breeds N Atlantic and Mediterranean. Migrates to S Atlantic and S Indian Oceans. One NZ record: Foxton Beach, January 1934.

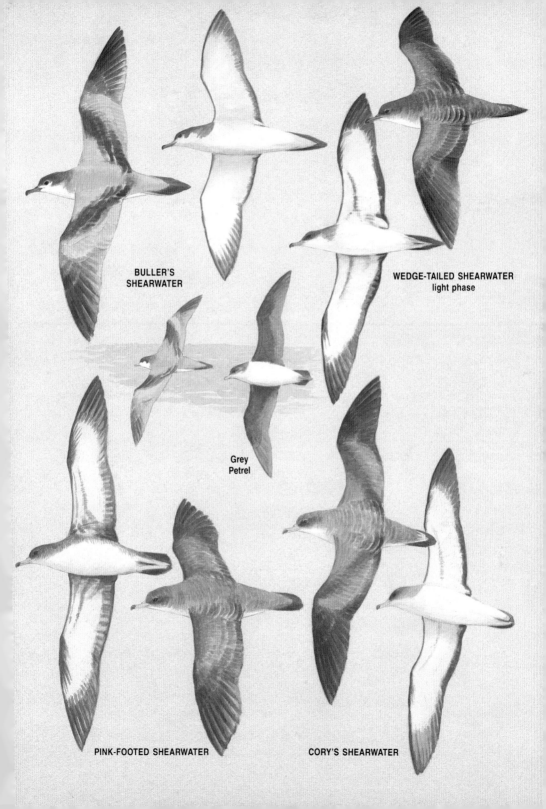

BULLER'S
SHEARWATER

WEDGE-TAILED SHEARWATER
light phase

Grey
Petrel

PINK-FOOTED SHEARWATER

CORY'S SHEARWATER

Plate 8

SHEARWATERS

SOOTY SHEARWATER (Titi, Muttonbird) *Puffinus griseus* Abundant native

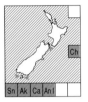

44 cm, 800 g. Sooty-brown upperparts, slightly greyer underparts with *silvery-grey flash on underwings*. Wings long and narrow, tail short and rounded. Bill long and slender (42 x 13 mm), dark grey; feet dark lilac with brown markings on the outer side. Main call a series of hoarse moans: 'oo-oo-ah', getting louder and faster each time. **Habitat:** Breeds mainly around NZ, on islands and mainland headlands from Three Kings to Campbell Is, but also southern Australia, Macquarie I and southern S America. Main NZ colonies are at The Snares, islands off Stewart Island and in Foveaux Strait, and Chatham Is. NZ birds migrate to N Pacific, many becoming beach-wrecked in Apr–May and Oct–Dec. **Breeding:** Nov–May.

SHORT-TAILED SHEARWATER *Puffinus tenuirostris* Common Australian migrant

42 cm, 550 g. Like small Sooty Shearwater but shorter-billed (32 x 11 mm) and *underwings are normally dull grey and do not flash prominently*. Feet dark lilac with brown markings on the outer side. **Habitat:** Breeds southern Australia, especially on islands in Bass Strait. Migrates to N Pacific, but some pass through NZ waters on the outward and return journeys, and are often beach-wrecked around May and October.

WEDGE-TAILED SHEARWATER *Puffinus pacificus* Locally common native

46 cm, 450 g. Variable plumages but always with *broad wings and long wedge-shaped tail*. Common dark phase all blackish brown except for slightly paler but *nonreflective* centres to underwing. Bill compressed (38 x 13 mm), slate grey; legs and feet pale flesh. See Plate 7 for pale phase. Main ground call a wailing moan: 'ka-whooo-ahh'. **Habitat:** Subtropical and tropical Pacific and Indian Oceans. Breeds on Kermadec Is and rarely reaches NZ mainland. **Breeding:** Dec–Jun.

CHRISTMAS ISLAND SHEARWATER *Puffinus nativitatis* Rare tropical vagrant

38 cm, 350 g. Completely sooty brown. Like Sooty Shearwater and Short-tailed Shearwater but much smaller; *dark brown underwing* and longer slightly wedge-shaped tail. Bill long and slender (40 x 10 mm), black; *feet dark brown*. **Habitat:** Breeds tropical and subtropical mid-Pacific Ocean. Two NZ records: Dargaville Beach, February 1976; Curtis I (Kermadecs) November 1989.

FLESH-FOOTED SHEARWATER *Puffinus carneipes* Common native

44 cm, 600 g. Large, bulky chocolate-brown shearwater with *pale bill (42 x 13 mm), darker at tip, and flesh-pink legs and feet*. Main call a series of high-pitched moans, resembling sound of cats fighting. **Habitat:** Breeds in western Indian Ocean, southern Australia, Lord Howe I, northern NZ and in Cook Strait. Main NZ colonies at Hen and Chickens, Mercury group, Karewa I, Saddleback I (near New Plymouth), and Trio and Titi Is (Cook Strait). Ranges through coastal waters of North I, occasionally south to Foveaux Strait in the west and Banks Peninsula to Chathams in the east. Migrates to N Pacific. **Breeding:** Nov–May.

SOOTY SHEARWATER

SHORT-TAILED SHEARWATER

WEDGE-TAILED
SHEARWATER
dark phase

FLESH-FOOTED
SHEARWATER

CHRISTMAS ISLAND
SHEARWATER

Plate 9 # SHEARWATERS and DIVING PETRELS

FLUTTERING SHEARWATER (Pakaha) *Puffinus gavia* Abundant endemic

33 cm, 300 g. Head to below eye, upperparts and thigh patch dark greyish brown *merging into* white underparts and flank patch; faintly mottled partial collar; *underwings white* with brownish borders and dusky-grey armpits. Bill fine (33 x 9 mm). Like Hutton's Shearwater at sea but smaller; *paler underwings*. In hand, *sides of undertail coverts white*. Main call at colony a rapid staccato 'ka-how ka-how ka-how ka-how kehek kehek kehek kehek-errr'. **Habitat:** Breeds on many islands around North I and Cook Strait. Flocks common in coastal waters and harbours; some, especially juveniles, visit Australian waters in non-breeding season. **Breeding:** Sep–Feb.

HUTTON'S SHEARWATER *Puffinus huttoni* Locally common endemic

36 cm, 350 g. Head to below eye, upperparts and thigh patch blackish brown *merging into* white underparts and flank patch; faintly mottled broad collar; *underwings centred off-white with indistinct broad brownish borders and extensive dusky-grey armpits*. Bill (37 x 9 mm). Like Fluttering Shearwater at sea but larger; *darker underwings*. In hand, *sides of undertail coverts brown*. Main colony call 'ko-uw ko-uw ko-uw ko-uw, kee kee kee kee – aaah'. **Habitat:** Breeds only in Seaward Kaikoura Range. In NZ waters, mainly off east coast South I and in Cook Strait but migrates to Australian waters in winter. **Breeding:** Oct–Apr.

MANX SHEARWATER *Puffinus puffinus* Rare Atlantic vagrant

36 cm, 450 g. Head to below eye, and upperparts dark brownish black, *sharply demarcated* from white underparts; notch of white on upper neck. *Underwings, including armpits, white with sharply defined black edges and tips*. Bill slender (35 x 8 mm). **Habitat:** Breeds N Atlantic. Two NZ records.

LITTLE SHEARWATER *Puffinus assimilis* Common native

30 cm, 200 g. Head to *above* eye, and upperparts dark bluish black; eyebrow, face and underparts white; underwing white except for thin black border on trailing edge. Bill slender (25 x 8 mm), dull lead blue with black ridge and tip; *legs and feet pale blue* with fleshy webs. **Habitat:** Breeds widely in Atlantic and southern oceans. Main NZ colonies at Kermadecs, off Northland, Mercury Is, Chathams and Antipodes. Mostly sedentary but rarely seen in coastal waters. **Breeding:** Jul–Jan.

Diving petrels are small stocky seabirds with short broad wings, short wide bill and paired nostrils opening upwards; blue legs. Sexes alike. Fast whirring flight close to the surface. Generally coastal. Do not follow ships or trawlers. Noisy at night over and at breeding colonies.

COMMON DIVING PETREL (Kuaka) *Pelecanoides urinatrix* Abundant native

20 cm, 130 g. Upperparts black; sides of face, neck and throat mottled grey; underparts white but underwings smoky grey. Bill stubby (16 x 8 mm), black; blue legs and feet. Like South Georgian Diving Petrel at sea but underwing darker. In hand, underwing coverts greyish brown, inner webs of *3 outer primaries dusky brown, and septal process near base of nostril*. **Habitat:** Breeds circumpolar subantarctic. Main NZ sites off eastern North I, Cook and Foveaux Straits, Chatham Is, The Snares, Antipodes and Auckland Is. **Breeding:** Aug–Feb.

SOUTH GEORGIAN DIVING PETREL *Pelecanoides georgicus* Rare native

18 cm, 120 g. Like Common Diving Petrel at sea, but underwing usually paler. In hand, underwing coverts white, inner webs of *3 outer primaries white or pale grey, septal process in bill near centre of nostril*. **Habitat:** Breeds circumpolar subantarctic; in NZ region, only on Codfish I, off Stewart I. **Breeding:** Nov–Mar.

FLUTTERING
SHEARWATER

HUTTON'S
SHEARWATER

Subantarctic

MANX
SHEARWATER

LITTLE SHEARWATER

COMMON DIVING PETREL

SOUTH GEORGIAN DIVING PETREL

Plate 10

PROCELLARIA PETRELS

Large heavy-bodied seabirds with robust pale and well-hooked bill; prominent nostrils encased in a tube. Sexes and ages alike. In flight, long glides on stiffly held wings with occasional wingbeats. When windy, soar and wheel in huge arcs. Dive into sea and swim underwater with wings. Generally oceanic; rarely seen near land. Most follow ships and fishing boats. Clumsy on ground; legs and webbed feet set well back. Generally silent over breeding grounds at night, but loud calls and clacks from ground and burrows. Lay 1 large white egg, usually deep in a burrow. Long incubation and fledging periods.

Flesh-footed Shearwater (see Plate 8)

WHITE-CHINNED PETREL (Shoemaker) *Procellaria aequinoctialis*
Uncommon native

55 cm, 1250 g. Entirely dark blackish brown except for a *variable amount of white feathering on chin*. Bill (52 x 21 mm) yellowish horn, *without dark tip*, but dark nostrils and lines between plates; legs and feet black. Sometimes follows ships and fishing boats. **Habitat:** Breeds circumpolar subantarctic, including Antipodes, Auckland and Campbell Is. Occasionally seen near mainland NZ but mainly ranges to the south and east. **Breeding:** Nov–May.

WESTLAND PETREL *Procellaria westlandica*
Uncommon endemic

48 cm, 1100 g. Entirely dark blackish brown. Bill (49 x 20 mm) yellowish horn *with dark tip* and black between the plates; legs and feet black. Like Black Petrel but larger. Often follows ships and fishing boats. **Habitat:** Breeds in the forested coastal foothills of the Paparoa Range between Barrytown and Punakaiki, West Coast. In breeding season, seen mainly off east coast from East Cape to Banks Peninsula, Cook Strait and off west coast from Fiordland to Taranaki, but ranges west to Australia. Migrates to central or eastern S Pacific, Dec–Mar. **Breeding:** May–Dec.

BLACK PETREL (Taiko) *Procellaria parkinsoni*
Uncommon endemic

46 cm, 700 g. Entirely dark blackish brown. Bill (41 x 15 mm) bluish yellow *with dark tip* and black between the plates; legs and feet black. Like Westland Petrel but smaller. Often follows ships and fishing boats. **Habitat:** Breeds only on Little Barrier and Great Barrier Is; formerly on inland ranges of the mainland. In breeding season, seen mainly around North I and west to Australia. Migrates to eastern tropical Pacific, Jul–Oct. **Breeding:** Nov–Jun.

GREY PETREL (Pediunker) *Procellaria cinerea*
Uncommon native

48 cm, 1000 g. Head and sides of face to below eye dark grey; upperparts ashy grey, darker on tail and wings, *merging* into white underparts without any strongly defined line; *dark grey underwings and undertail* separate it from large grey and white shearwaters (see Plate 7). Bill stout (47 x 17 mm), greenish flesh with black between plates and on nostrils; legs and feet greyish flesh, darker on outside, yellowish webs. Distinctive albatross-like gliding with rapid duck-like wingbeats. Regularly follows ships and fishing boats. **Habitat:** Breeds circumpolar subantarctic; in NZ region, at Antipodes and Campbell Is. Rarely seen near NZ mainland. **Breeding:** Feb–Nov.

Flesh-footed
Shearwater

WHITE-CHINNED PETREL

WESTLAND PETREL

BLACK PETREL

GREY PETREL

Plate 11 FULMARINE PETRELS and BLUE PETREL

A diverse group of distinctive medium to large seabirds. Sexes alike. Most breed at high latitudes and lay 1 white egg, mostly in a scrape on ledges, in crevices or rockfalls; the exceptions being giant petrels (Plate 6), which lay in a cupped mound, and Kerguelen Petrels (Plate 15), which nest in a burrow.

ANTARCTIC PETREL *Thalassoica antarctica* — Locally common native

45 cm, 650 g. Head, neck, back and rump dark brown; *upperwings dark brown with broad white trailing edge and inner part of primaries*; tail white, tipped brown; underparts white; underwing white with black leading edge and thin border. Bill dark olive brown (black in juvenile); legs and feet greyish flesh. **Habitat:** Breeds circumpolar Antarctica, sometimes well inland; in NZ region, at Rockefeller Mts, Scott I and possibly Balleny Is. Ranges through Antarctic waters; especially common in Ross Sea sector. In winter, few reach NZ mainland waters but sometimes present in moderate numbers. **Breeding:** Nov–Mar.

ANTARCTIC FULMAR *Fulmarus glacialoides* — Locally common native

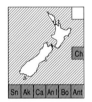

50 cm, 800 g. Head, neck and underparts white; mantle, back, rump and tail pearly grey; *upperwings pearly grey with darker grey trailing edge, and primaries black with large white patch near wingtip*. Bill strong (45 mm), pinkish horn with blue tinge on nasal tubes, and black tip; legs and feet pinkish blue. Appears large-headed; glides on stiff wings. **Habitat:** Breeds circumpolar on coast of Antarctica and subantarctic islands of Atlantic Ocean; in NZ region, at Balleny Is. Ranges widely in southern oceans, and a few visit NZ waters in winter and spring, but sometimes many are beach-wrecked in spring. **Breeding:** Dec–Apr.

CAPE PIGEON *Daption capense* — Common native

40 cm, 450 g. Head, neck and mantle black; lower back, base of upperwing and rump white, heavily chequered with black; outer upperwing black with broad white patches near body and beyond bend of wing; white tail is flecked black and broadly tipped black; underparts white; underwings white with black leading edge and thin borders. Bill stout (30 x 15 mm), black; legs and feet black. Snares Cape Pigeon (*australe*) has less white on upperparts than Southern Cape Pigeon (*capense*). Often follows ships and gathers around fishing boats. **Habitat:** Breeds circumpolar subantarctic and coast of Antarctica; in NZ region, as far north as The Snares and Chathams. Ranges widely through southern oceans and common off NZ mainland, especially in winter. **Breeding:** Nov–Apr.

BLUE PETREL *Halobaena caerulea* — Uncommon subantarctic visitor

29 cm, 200 g. Head bluish black; upperparts and side of neck pale blue, with dark M-shaped mark from wingtip to wingtip, broken only on lower back; *tail distinctively tipped white*. Bill narrow (27 x 11 mm), bluish black; legs and feet blue with flesh webs. At sea, looks like a prion (see Plate 12), but white-tipped tail distinctive and flight faster and wheeling. Rarely follows ships. **Habitat:** Breeds circumpolar subantarctic; nearest colony to NZ is on Macquarie I. Uncommon winter and spring visitor to waters around NZ mainland but sometimes beach-wrecked in moderate numbers.

SNOW PETREL *Pagodroma nivea* — Locally common native

35 cm, 325 g. *All white*. Bill narrow (22 x 11 mm), black; legs and feet black. Flight erratic with short, rapid wingbeats. **Habitat:** Breeds circumpolar coast of Antarctica; in NZ region, at Balleny Is (Greater Snow Petrel *nivea*) and around Ross Sea (Lesser Snow Petrel *minor*). Ranges through southern oceans but never confirmed as far north as NZ mainland. **Breeding:** Nov–Apr.

ANTARCTIC PETREL

ANTARCTIC FULMAR

CAPE PIGEON

Snares

Southern

BLUE PETREL

SNOW PETREL

Plate 12

PRIONS

Small seabirds with blue-grey upperparts with black M across upperwings and lower back, white underparts, black-tipped tail, and blue legs and feet. Bill has comb-like lamellae on inside. Sexes and ages alike. Species separated by size, bill structure, face colours and extent of black on tail. Flight fast, buoyant and erratic; usually stay close to the surface. Feed near surface by plunging or dipping. Generally oceanic. Do not follow ships or fishing boats. Noisy at night at breeding colonies, with harsh cooing and cackling calls in air or on ground.

FAIRY PRION (Titi Wainui)   *Pachyptila turtur*   **Abundant native**

25 cm, 125 g. Upperparts blue-grey; faint white eyebrow; bold black M across wings; *tail broadly tipped black, including tips of uppertail coverts.* Bill (22 x 11 mm) blue with large nail. **Habitat:** Breeds circumpolar subantarctic, including many islands around NZ, especially Poor Knights, Cook Strait, Motunau I, Foveaux Strait, The Snares and Chathams. Abundant in coastal waters near breeding colonies, and the most common beach-wrecked bird. Ranges through Tasman Sea and east of NZ. **Breeding:** Nov–Feb.

FULMAR PRION   *Pachyptila crassirostris*   **Locally common native**

26 cm, 140 g. Like Fairy Prion but slightly larger and paler. Bill (23 x 11 mm) deeper and with very large nail. **Habitat**: Breeds subantarctic at Heard I (S Indian Ocean), Chathams (Pyramid, Forty Fours), Bounty, The Snares and Auckland Is. Probably mainly sedentary but occasionally reaches NZ coast. **Breeding:** Nov–Feb.

BROAD-BILLED PRION (Parara)   *Pachyptila vittata*   **Common native**

28 cm, 200 g. Upperparts blue-grey; black M across wings; dark face with clear white eyebrow; *very narrow black tip to tail. Bill very broad* (34 x 20 mm), *iron-grey.* **Habitat:** Breeds S Atlantic and around southern NZ; main colonies are in Fiordland, Foveaux Strait, off Stewart I, The Snares and Chathams. Ranges around NZ coast and rarely to Australia. **Breeding:** Aug–Jan.

THIN-BILLED PRION   *Pachyptila belcheri*   **Common visitor**

26 cm, 145 g. *Upperparts pale blue-grey; indistinct blackish M across wings; very pale face with prominent white eyebrow; very narrow black tip to tail. Bill slender* (25 x 11 mm) with weak hook. **Habitat:** Breeds subantarctic S America, Falklands and Indian Ocean. Ranges through southern oceans in winter and spring, regularly reaching NZ.

SALVIN'S PRION   *Pachyptila salvini*   **Common visitor**

27 cm, 170 g. Upperparts blue-grey, *slightly darker on the head;* blackish M across wings; *narrow black tip to tail.* Bill stout (30 x 16 mm), bluish. Like Antarctic Prion, but in the hand, bill larger and *lamellae visible* at base of closed bill. **Habitat:** Breeds in subantarctic Indian Ocean. Regular visitor to NZ seas in winter and spring.

ANTARCTIC PRION   *Pachyptila desolata*   **Locally common native**

26 cm, 150 g. Like Salvin's Prion, but in the hand, bill smaller (27 x 14 mm) and *lamellae not visible* at the base of the closed bill. **Habitat:** Breeds widely in subantarctic and antarctic zones; in NZ region, many breed at Auckland Is and a few nest at Scott Is, Ross Sea. Regular visitor to seas off NZ mainland, mainly in winter and spring. **Breeding:** Dec–Mar.

Blue Petrel (see Plate 11)

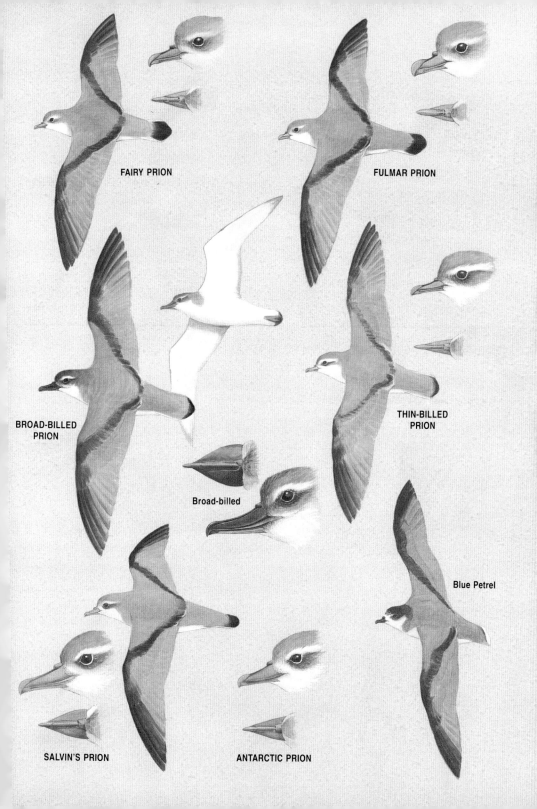

FAIRY PRION

FULMAR PRION

BROAD-BILLED
PRION

THIN-BILLED
PRION

Broad-billed

Blue Petrel

SALVIN'S PRION

ANTARCTIC PRION

Plate 13   GADFLY PETRELS

Medium to large seabirds with mostly short deep and heavily hooked bill, nostrils encased in a tube, joined at the base of the bill. Most are dark above and mainly white below. Sexes and ages alike; males slightly larger. Underwing patterns are often distinctive. In flight, long narrow wings held stiffly and appear graceful as they glide and wheel in huge arcs. Generally oceanic; rarely seen near land. Many species highly migratory. Many species give high-pitched repetitive calls over breeding grounds at night. Lay 1 large egg, usually deep in a burrow. Long incubation and fledging periods.

COOK'S PETREL (Titi) *Pterodroma cookii*   Uncommon endemic

29 cm, 200 g. Forehead white, scaled grey on forecrown; dark eye patch; crown and upperparts pale grey with dark M across wings. Underparts and underwings white except mottled black patch at bend of wing extending towards tip and as short diagonal line a short way towards body. Bill long and fine (28 x 10 mm), black; legs and feet bluish with yellowish base of webs, dark toes and ends to webs. **Habitat:** Breeds Little Barrier, Great Barrier and Codfish Is. Migrates to eastern Pacific, from California to Chile. **Breeding:** Oct–May.

PYCROFT'S PETREL *Pterodroma pycrofti*   Rare endemic

28 cm, 160 g. Forehead and forecrown white scaled with grey; crown, hindneck and sides of face to under eye medium grey *(paler than Stejneger's Petrel but darker than Cook's Petrel); upperparts medium grey* with dark M across wings. Underparts and underwings white except for mottled black patch at bend of wing extending towards tip and as short diagonal line a short way towards body. Bill short and fine (24 x 9 mm), black; legs and feet bluish with darker toes and ends to webs. **Habitat:** Breeds northeastern NZ; main colonies at Mercury, Hen and Chickens, and Poor Knights Is. Occasionally beach-wrecked, mainly in northern NZ in summer and autumn. Migrates to central N Pacific. **Breeding:** Nov–Apr.

GOULD'S PETREL *Pterodroma leucoptera*   Uncommon subtropical visitor

29 cm, 175 g. Forehead white; *black crown, sides of face, nape and sides of neck to wing*; rest of upperparts grey with darker M across wings. Underparts and underwings white except for black patch at bend of wing extending towards tip and as thick diagonal bar well towards body. Bill short and fine (24 x 10 mm), black; legs and feet bluish with dark toes and ends to webs. **Habitat:** Breeds Cabbage Tree I (NSW) and New Caledonia. The latter birds range through Tasman Sea and to NZ waters. Migrates to eastern tropical Pacific.

STEJNEGER'S PETREL *Pterodroma longirostris*   Rare subtropical vagrant

28 cm, 150 g. Like Gould's Petrel except smaller and black cap is reduced with *white on forecrown; grey neck and sides of neck*; diagonal bar on underwing less prominent. **Habitat:** Breeds at Mas-a-fuera, Juan Fernandez group, off Chile. Migrates to subtropical N Pacific. Vagrants occasionally reach NZ in summer.

Black-winged Petrel (see Plate 14)

COOK'S PETREL

PYCROFT'S PETREL

STEJNEGER'S
PETREL

GOULD'S PETREL

Black-winged Petrel

Plate 14

GADFLY PETRELS

WHITE-NAPED PETREL   *Pterodroma cervicalis*   Uncommon endemic

43 cm, 450 g. Forehead white; blackish cap on crown, nape and sides of face to below eye; *broad white collar across hindneck*; upperparts frosty grey with broad black M across wings; small grey tab in front of wings. Underparts and underwing white except for black patch at bend of wing extending towards tip and diagonally towards body. Bill sturdy (37 x 16 mm), black; feet and legs fleshy pink with black toes and ends of webs. **Habitat:** Breeds Macauley I, Kermadecs. Migrates to subtropical N Pacific, mainly in the west. A few vagrants reach waters off mainland NZ. **Breeding:** Dec–Jun.

JUAN FERNANDEZ PETREL   *Pterodroma externa*   Rare subtropical vagrant

43 cm, 500 g. Like White-naped Petrel except hindneck grey, cap is paler and underwings have only a short black tab extending from bend of wing towards body. **Habitat:** Breeds Mas-a-fuera, Juan Fernandez group, off Chile. Migrates to subtropical N Pacific. A few vagrants reach NZ waters.

MOTTLED PETREL (Korure)   *Pterodroma inexpectata*   Common endemic

34 cm, 325 g. *Face white, heavily mottled grey;* upperparts dark frosty grey, with darker M across wings; dark eye patch; *underparts white except grey patch on the lower breast and belly.* Underwing white with broad black diagonal band from bend of wing to near body. Bill small (27 x 12 mm), black; legs and feet fleshy pink with black toes and ends of webs. **Habitat:** Breeds Fiordland, Codfish I and other islands off Stewart I, and at The Snares. Ranges to pack ice, around NZ mainland and to Chathams in breeding season. Migrates to N Pacific. **Breeding:** Dec–Jun.

BLACK-WINGED PETREL   *Pterodroma nigripennis*   Common native

30 cm, 175 g. Forehead white, mottled on forecrown; dark patch below eye; crown, sides of neck and upperparts pale grey; upperwings grey with darker M across wings. Underparts and underwings white except for dark outer half to primaries, dark trailing edge and *black diagonal band from bend of wing to near body.* Bill short and stubby (24 x 11 mm), black; legs and feet fleshy pink with dark toes and ends to webs. **Habitat:** Breeds subtropical S Pacific, including Kermadecs, Three Kings, East, Portland and Chatham Is. Seen prospecting over headlands on northern NZ coast. Migrates to N Pacific. **Breeding:** Dec–Jun.

CHATHAM PETREL   *Pterodroma axillaris*   Rare endemic

30 cm, 200 g. Like Black-winged Petrel, but underwing has only tips of primaries dark, narrow dark trailing edge, but *black diagonal bar reaches to black base of underwing.* **Habitat:** Breeds only at South East I, Chathams. **Breeding:** Dec–Jun.

WHITE-NAPED PETREL

JUAN FERNANDEZ PETREL

MOTTLED PETREL

BLACK-WINGED PETREL

CHATHAM PETREL

Plate 15

GADFLY PETRELS

WHITE-HEADED PETREL *Pterodroma lessonii* **Locally common native**

43 cm, 600 g. *Head mainly white with dark eye patch* and very faintly grey on crown and hindneck; pale grey on back and tail; upperwings greyish brown with indistinct M joining across lower back; *underwings dark grey, undertail white.* Bill stout (37 x 15 mm), black; legs and feet fleshy pink with brown on outer toe, joints of toes and ends of webs. Flight strong and rapid, wheeling and swooping in high arcs. Rarely follows ships. **Habitat:** Breeds subantarctic in Indian Ocean and Macquarie I; in NZ region, at Antipodes and Auckland Is. Ranges through southern oceans between pack ice and about 34°S in winter. Regularly recorded beach-wrecked on west coast of North I. **Breeding:** Nov–May.

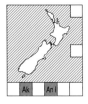

KERGUELEN PETREL *Lugensa brevirostris* **Uncommon subantarctic visitor**

33 cm, 350 g. Almost uniformly *dark frosty grey*, with slight mottling on forehead, chin and sometimes flanks; underwings silvery grey. *Bill short and narrow* (26 x 10 mm), black; looks small compared to large head. Legs and feet purplish flesh, darker on outsides. Flight extremely fast. **Habitat:** Breeds subantarctic in Atlantic and Indian Oceans. Ranges eastwards and can be quite common in the Tasman Sea some years in winter and early spring, when sometimes wrecked on west coast NZ beaches.

PROVIDENCE PETREL *Pterodroma solandri* **Rare subtropical vagrant**

40 cm, 500 g. Brown head, mottled white on face and forehead and dark patch in front of eye; upperparts steely grey, contrasting with browner wings and tail; underparts greyish brown; underwings dark grey with distinctive *white patch at the base of dark primaries.* Bill stout (35 x 15 mm), black; legs and feet dark grey. **Habitat:** Breeds in winter at Lord Howe and Philip Is; formerly also at Norfolk I. Migrates to N Pacific. Two beach-wrecked birds recorded in NZ.

GREY-FACED PETREL (Oi) *Pterodroma macroptera* **Common native**

41 cm, 550 g. *Entire plumage blackish brown except pale grey forehead, sides of face, chin and throat.* Bill stout (36 x 14 mm), black; legs and feet black. Long narrow wings. Flight strong and rapid, wheeling and swooping in big arcs. Aerial chases at dusk or after dark over breeding colonies often accompanied by *'o-hi'* or *'o-hoe'* calls. Many calls also from birds on ground or in burrows, especially a loud 'or-wik' and 'si-si-si'. **Habitat:** Breeds circumpolar subantarctic and southern temperate; in NZ, on many northern offshore islands and some mainland cliffs and headlands, within the triangle Cape Egmont to Three Kings Is to Gisborne. **Breeding:** Jun–Jan.

KERMADEC PETREL *Pterodroma neglecta* **Locally common native**

38 cm, 500 g. Variable plumages. Dark phase is uniformly brownish black except for *obvious white bases to the primaries on underwing,* and white inner webs and shafts of primaries sometimes visible on upperwing. Bill (30 x 13 mm) black; feet and legs variable from black to pale flesh with dark tips to webs. See Plate 16 for other phases. **Habitat:** Breeds subtropical S Pacific, including Kermadec Is. Migrates to tropical Pacific. Vagrants occasionally reach NZ mainland. **Breeding:** Oct–May.

WHITE-HEADED PETREL

KERGUELEN PETREL

PROVIDENCE PETREL

GREY-FACED PETREL

KERMADEC PETREL
dark phase

Plate 16   # GADFLY PETRELS

SOFT-PLUMAGED PETREL   *Pterodroma mollis*   Uncommon native

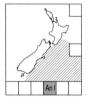

34 cm, 300 g. Head including patch below and behind eye greyish brown; forehead scaled white; eyebrow, chin, sides of neck and throat white. Upperparts slaty grey with a broad blackish band across wing coverts; underparts white except for a *narrow grey band completely or partially across the chest; underwing grey*. Bill stout (35 x 12 mm), black; feet and legs pinkish with dark outer toe and tips to webs. **Habitat:** Breeds subantarctic in Atlantic and Indian Oceans, and at Antipodes Is. Ranges through southern oceans but not common in S Pacific, although increasing numbers seen off southern and eastern coasts of NZ since 1970s. **Breeding:** Dec–May.

CHATHAM ISLAND TAIKO (Magenta Petrel)   *Pterodroma magentae*   Rare endemic

38 cm, 475 g. Head, neck, upper breast and upperparts uniformly dark sooty grey except for variable greyish scalloping on forehead and grey chin; lower breast, underparts and undertail white; underwing sooty grey. Bill robust (32 x 16 mm), black; legs and feet pink with dark outer toe and tips to webs. **Habitat:** Breeds in forests of southern Chatham I. Assumed to migrate into subtropical Pacific. **Breeding:** Nov–May.

PHOENIX PETREL   *Pterodroma alba*   Rare tropical vagrant

35 cm, 275 g. Head, upperparts and upper breast uniform sooty brown; *chin and upper throat white*; breast, belly and undertail white except for narrow dark rim around tip of long tail; underwings sooty brown except for *thin white band just back from leading edge from body to bend of wing*. Bill slight (28 x 11 mm), black; legs and feet pink with dark outer toe and tips to webs. **Habitat:** Breeds tropical and subtropical Pacific; possibly formerly on Kermadec Is, where twice recorded.

TAHITI PETREL   *Pseudobulweria rostrata*   Rare tropical vagrant

38 cm, 400 g. Head, upperparts, chin, throat and upper breast uniform sooty brown; lower breast, belly and undertail white, except for *broad dark tip to long pointed tail*; underwings *uniformly* sooty brown. Bill massive (37 x 17 mm), black; legs mainly pink, feet mainly dark. **Habitat:** Breeds tropical and subtropical Pacific. One NZ specimen: Dargaville Beach, June 1988; but others seen in Bay of Plenty in winter 1988.

KERMADEC PETREL   *Pterodroma neglecta*   Locally common native

38 cm, 500 g. Variable plumages. Pale phase has head, neck and body white to pale ashy grey with flecks of grey or brown; upperwing brownish black except white inner webs and shaft of primaries sometimes visible; underwing dark greyish brown with *obvious white bases to the primaries*. Intermediate phase similar but has variable amounts of brown on head, upperparts, upper breast and undertail. See Plate 15 for dark phase. Bill (30 x 13 mm) black; feet and legs variable from black to pale flesh with dark tips to webs. **Habitat:** Breeds subtropical S Pacific, including Kermadec Is. Migrates to tropical Pacific. Vagrants occasionally reach NZ mainland. **Breeding:** Oct–May.

SOFT-PLUMAGED PETREL

CHATHAM ISLAND
TAIKO

KERMADEC
PETREL
light phase

ENIX PETREL

KERMADEC
PETREL
intermediate phase

TAHITI PETREL

Plate 17   **STORM PETRELS**

Very small dainty seabirds with broad rounded wings, short bill with a prominent nostril with a single opening, and very long legs. Mostly black or grey upperparts except for rump. Sexes and ages alike. Fly close to the surface, erratically with short glides or hops. Pick up food while hovering or pattering on the water. Oceanic; rarely follow boats. Most silent at night over colonies, but give coos, churrs or whistles from burrows or the ground.

WILSON'S STORM PETREL   *Oceanites oceanicus*   **Locally common native**

18 cm, 35 g. *Brownish black* with faint diagonal grey-brown bar on upperwing from bend of wing to body; prominent *unmarked white rump; square tail.* Yellow-webbed feet project beyond tail. **Habitat:** Breeds subantarctic and Antarctica, including several colonies in the Ross Sea Sector. Migrates to Northern Hemisphere but occasionally seen in NZ waters, mainly Nov–Dec and Mar–May. **Breeding:** Dec–Apr.

LEACH'S STORM PETREL   *Oceanodroma leucorhoa*   **Rare straggler**

20 cm, 45 g. *All blackish brown* except head darker, clear diagonal grey-brown bar on upperwing from bend of wing to body, *white rump with a dark central line; forked tail.* **Habitat:** Breeds N Pacific and N Atlantic. Migrates to tropics, but a few reach NZ waters.

GREY-BACKED STORM PETREL   *Oceanites nereis*   **Locally common native**

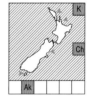

18 cm, 35 g. Head, neck, throat and upper breast greyish black, rest of underparts white; back, upperwings and tail ashy grey, with black tips to wings and square tail. **Habitat:** Breeds circumpolar subantarctic; in NZ region, at Chathams, Antipodes, Auckland and Campbell Is. Mainly sedentary but ranges to 30°S in NZ seas, though rarely seen near mainland coast. **Breeding:** Sep–Mar.

WHITE-FACED STORM PETREL (Takahikare-moana)   *Pelagodroma marina*
Common native

20 cm, 45 g. *Forehead, eyebrow and underparts white;* crown, nape and patch through eye dark grey brown; back and upperwing brownish grey, contrasting with pale grey (NZ subspecies) or white (Kermadec subspecies) rump; slightly forked black tail. **Habitat:** Breeds temperate and subtropical Atlantic and around Australia and NZ; main NZ colonies in Hauraki Gulf, Bay of Plenty, Motunau I, around Stewart and Auckland Is and Chathams. Disperses widely after breeding and rarely seen in NZ coastal waters. **Breeding:** Oct–Mar.

BLACK-BELLIED STORM PETREL   *Fregetta tropica*   **Locally common native**

20 cm, 55 g. Variable; some almost identical to White-bellied Storm Petrel, but *feet project well beyond tail.* Typically has black upperparts except broad *white rump*, grey chin and *variable black line down centre of white belly* connecting black breast and undertail. A few have all white belly. **Habitat:** Breeds circumpolar subantarctic, including Antipodes and Auckland Is. Ranges widely and migrates to tropics in winter. **Breeding:** Dec–Apr.

WHITE-BELLIED STORM PETREL   *Fregetta grallaria*   **Rare native**

20 cm, 50 g. Variable plumages; some like a few Black-bellied Storm Petrels, but *feet level with tip of tail.* Typically has black upperparts, mantle feathers often white-tipped; *rump white*; black chin, throat and breast contrasts with *white belly*; black undertail. Some have smudgy, not white, underwings. **Habitat:** Breeds subtropics, including Kermadecs. Ranges widely at sea but rarely seen off NZ coast. **Breeding:** Jan–Jun.

WILSON'S
STORM PETREL

LEACH'S
STORM PETREL

GREY-BACKED
STORM PETREL

WHITE-FACED
STORM PETREL

BLACK-BELLIED STORM PETREL

WHITE-BELLIED STORM PETREL

Plate 18   **PENGUINS**

Flightless stocky seabirds with dark upperparts and white underparts. Wings modified into flippers. Robust bill. Short stout legs with webbed feet. Dense short and flattened feathers in adults; thick down in chicks. Swim low in the water, with head and upper back (occasionally tail) visible; some porpoise when swimming fast. Feed at sea by diving. On land, walk upright with waddling gait or short hops with flippers used to maintain balance. Toboggan on ice and mud. Visit land to breed and to moult. During the 2–6-week moult, birds look ragged while all feathers are replaced rapidly; birds fast and are unable to swim. Breed solitarily in burrows or under vegetation, or in large dense colonies on the surface. Lay 1–2 white eggs.

KING PENGUIN   *Aptenodytes patagonicus*   Uncommon subantarctic visitor

90 cm, 13 kg. Glossy black head and sides of face; *golden-orange comma-shaped wedge behind eye* tapering towards orange upper breast; silver-grey nape, shading to blue-grey on back and darker margin on flanks; rest of underparts white. Bill long and decurved at tip; broad tapering panel of orange-pink at base of lower mandible. Juvenile similar but much paler yellow, bill patch small and pink, and *dark chin and throat*. **Habitat:** Breeds circumpolar in subantarctic; nearest colony to NZ at Macquarie I. Ranges south to pack ice; regularly seen at NZ subantarctic islands in summer and autumn, but only vagrants reach NZ mainland.

EMPEROR PENGUIN   *Aptenodytes forsteri*   Uncommon native

115 cm, 30 kg. Head, chin and throat blackish blue; *orange patch extending downward from behind eye towards the back*, connected to lemon-yellow upper breast; upperparts bluish grey with darker border along flanks; underparts white. Bill long and decurved towards tip; tapering panel of lilac-pink at base of lower mandible. Juvenile lacks yellow and has *white chin and throat*. **Habitat:** Breeds circumpolar in large colonies around Antarctica, including Ross Dependency. Rare vagrants reach NZ mainland. **Breeding:** Apr–Jan.

MAGELLANIC PENGUIN   *Spheniscus magellanicus*   Rare South American vagrant

70 cm, 3.5 kg. Upperparts blue-black; wide white crescent from above bill, behind eye to upper breast separates crown and nape from black face and chin; two black bands cross upper breast, the narrower lower one horseshoe-shaped, turning down sides of belly to near feet. Juvenile has less clearly marked face pattern and a smudgy breast band. **Habitat:** Breeds on coast of S America. Rare vagrant to NZ.

GENTOO PENGUIN   *Pygoscelis papua*   Rare subantarctic vagrant

75 cm, 5.5 kg. Upperparts, chin and throat dark slate grey; *white triangle above each eye, connected by thin white line over top of head*; scattered white spots on head and neck; underparts white. Bill black with sides orange (male) or pinkish orange (female). Juvenile similar, but throat pale and patches over eye do not connect over crown. **Habitat:** Breeds circumpolar subantarctic and Antarctica; nearest colony to NZ at Macquarie I. Vagrants reach NZ subantarctic islands and occasionally NZ mainland.

juv

KING PENGUIN

juv

EMPEROR PENGUIN

MAGELLANIC PENGUIN

moulting

GENTOO PENGUIN

Plate 19

PENGUINS

YELLOW-EYED PENGUIN (Hoiho) *Megadyptes antipodes* Uncommon endemic

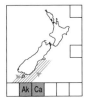

65 cm, 5.4 kg. Upperparts slaty grey; *forehead, crown and sides of face pale golden yellow* with black feather shafts; eye yellow. Adult has *band of yellow feathers starting at eye and encircling back of head.* Juvenile has greyer head and lacks yellow band. **Habitat:** Breeds and moults around southeastern South I, Foveaux Strait, Stewart, Codfish, Campbell and Auckland Is. Mainly sedentary, but some disperse northwards to Cook Strait, occasionally further. **Breeding:** Sep–Mar.

ADÉLIE PENGUIN *Pygoscelis adeliae* Locally common native

70 cm, 5 kg. Black head, face, chin and upperparts, except conspicuous *white eye-ring;* underparts white; *no crest.* Juvenile similar but has white chin and sides to face to just below the eye. **Habitat:** Breeds circumpolar in large colonies in Antarctica, including Ross Dependency. Rare vagrants reach NZ mainland. **Breeding:** Nov–Feb.

CHINSTRAP PENGUIN *Pygoscelis antarctica* Rare native

75 cm, 5.5 kg. Black upperparts; sides of face from above eye, chin and underparts white, except for a *narrow black band extending diagonally across face* from behind eye to under throat. Juvenile has dusky face above facial band. **Habitat:** Breeds Antarctica from Antarctic Peninsula eastwards to Ross Dependency. Rare vagrants reach NZ mainland. **Breeding:** Nov–Mar.

BLUE PENGUIN (Korora) *Eudyptula minor* Common native

40 cm, 1100 g. Smallest penguin. *Slate-blue upperparts* and sides of face to near eye, white below; lacks crest or distinctive face markings. Juvenile has a brighter blue back. White-flippered phase, of Canterbury, has more white on upperside of flipper. Often noisy on land at night; utters loud screams, wails, trumpeting and deep growls. **Habitat:** Breeds on rocky coasts and islands throughout NZ, but nest can be several hundred metres inland. When breeding, comes ashore at dusk and departs at dawn. Moults in burrows, under rock piles or in dense vegetation; often surrounded by piles of moulted feathers. Often seen in coastal waters. **Breeding:** Aug–Mar.

YELLOW-EYED PENGUIN

moulting

juv

ADÉLIE PENGUIN

juv

juv

BLUE PENGUIN

CHINSTRAP PENGUIN

white-flippered phase

Plate 20   **PENGUINS**

FIORDLAND CRESTED PENGUIN (Tawaki)   *Eudyptes pachyrhynchus*

Rare endemic

60 cm, 4 kg. Upperparts dark bluish grey, darker on head; sides of face, chin and throat dark slaty grey; broad yellow eyebrow stripe that *splays out and droops* down neck; most have *3–6 whitish stripes on cheeks*. Little black on tip of underflipper. Moderately large orange bill with *no bare skin at base*. Juvenile has thin eyebrow, and whitish chin and throat. **Habitat:** Breeds and moults in dense coastal forest or in caves on rocky shores of southern NZ, mainly S Westland, Fiordland and Codfish I. During breeding, stays close to shore over continental shelf. Stragglers recorded around NZ coast and subantarctic islands. **Breeding:** Jul–Dec.

SNARES CRESTED PENGUIN   *Eudyptes robustus*

Locally common endemic

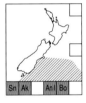

60 cm, 3 kg. Head, throat and upperparts dark blue-black; underparts white. *Thin bright yellow eyebrow stripe forms bushy drooping crest behind eye. Prominent pink skin at base of heavy* reddish-brown bill. Solid black tip to underflipper. Juvenile has smaller and creamy crest, darker bill and mottled whitish throat. **Habitat:** Breeds only at The Snares. Straggles to other subantarctic islands and mainland NZ. **Breeding:** Sep–Feb.

ERECT-CRESTED PENGUIN   *Eudyptes sclateri*

Locally common endemic

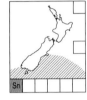

60 cm, 4.5 kg. Forehead, sides of face, chin and throat jet black; crown and upperparts very dark bluish black; underparts white. *Broad* bright yellow eyebrow stripe rises at a *steep angle over eye to form a short brush-like erectile crest* on each side of crown. Whitish skin at base of slender reddish-brown bill. Solid black tip to underflipper, extending well along leading edge. Juvenile has smaller and creamy crest, and throat mottled grey and white. **Habitat:** Breeds NZ subantarctic; main colonies at Bounty and Antipodes Is. After breeding, disperses widely; a few moult each autumn on NZ mainland coast, and regularly seen off NZ mainland in winter. **Breeding:** Oct–Feb.

ROCKHOPPER PENGUIN   *Eudyptes chrysocome*

Locally common native

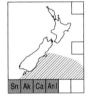

55 cm, 2.8 kg. Smallest crested penguin and has much smaller bill. Upperparts slate, darker on head, sides of face and chin. *Thin golden-yellow eyebrow stripe from either side of forehead* extending to splay at crown; some droop towards neck, others forming a *plume at edge of crest on hindcrown*. Juvenile similar but shorter crest, eyebrow stripe less well developed, and chin and throat streaked with ashy white. Size of crest, colour of bare skin at base of bill and pattern of black at underside tip of flipper used to separate subspecies. **Habitat:** Breeds circumpolar subantarctic; in NZ region, at Campbell, Auckland and Antipodes Is, often near or with Erect-crested Penguins. Stragglers reach The Snares, Chathams and NZ mainland. **Breeding:** Oct–Mar.

MACARONI PENGUIN   *Eudyptes chrysolophus*

Rare subantarctic straggler

70 cm, 4.5 kg. Largest crested penguin. Upperparts black; sides of face, chin and throat black in Macaroni form, but grey or white in Royal form. Both have *massive red-brown bill* with fleshy gape; yellow, golden orange and black *plumes starting from centre of forehead*. Juvenile has smaller tuft-like plumes. **Habitat:** Breeds Antarctica and subantarctic of S Atlantic and Indian Oceans (Macaroni) and at Macquarie I (Royal). Occasionally reaches NZ sector of Antarctica, NZ subantarctic islands and, rarely, the NZ mainland.

FIORDLAND CRESTED PENGUIN

SNARES CRESTED PENGUIN

juv

Eastern

Moseley's

ROCKHOPPER PENGUIN

ERECT-CRESTED
PENGUIN

Macaroni

Royal

MACARONI PENGUIN

Plate 21

TROPICBIRDS and FRIGATEBIRDS

Tropicbirds are medium-sized, white, rather tern-like seabirds mostly confined to the tropics. Distinguished from terns by their wedge-shaped tail. Sexes alike. Adults have 2 long central tail-streamers. Juveniles have black barring above and lack tail streamers. Their flight is distinctive; direct with strong steady wingbeats about 30 m above the sea. Over land, they ride the updraughts along cliffs and hills. At sea, they plunge-dive for fish and squid.

RED-TAILED TROPICBIRD (Amokura) *Phaethon rubricauda*   Rare tropical native

46 cm, (+ up to 40 cm for tail streamers), 800 g. Adult white with *black feather-shafts* on primaries, tertials and tail; black mark through eye. Tern-like *bright red bill*; tail streamers *red* but often difficult to see. Juvenile lacks tail streamers, is barred black above and has *black or dull red bill*. **Habitat:** Tropical seas; in NZ region, breeds at Kermadecs. Rare vagrant to northern NZ mainland. **Breeding:** Dec–Aug.

WHITE-TAILED TROPICBIRD *Phaethon lepturus*   Rare tropical vagrant

38 cm, (+ up to 40 cm for tail streamers), 300 g. Smaller and more graceful in flight than Red-tailed Tropicbird. Adult white with prominent *diagonal black band on inner wing and solid black patch near the tip of the upperwing*; tail streamers *white*; bill yellow to orange. Juvenile like that of Red-tailed Tropicbird but has black patch on the outer upperwing and pale yellow bill. **Habitat:** Tropical seas.

Frigatebirds are large dark seabirds with very long thin pointed wings, long deeply forked tail and long hooked bill. The sexes differ in the amount of white on their underparts; males are mostly black and have a dark bill, whereas females have a prominent white chest and a pale bill. Immatures are hard to separate, having gingery heads and white chests like females. Usually seen soaring high over tropical seas or pursuing other birds, particularly boobies and terns, forcing them to drop their food, which they catch in midair. They feed entirely on the wing, snatching flying fish and picking fish and squid from the surface of the sea.

LESSER FRIGATEBIRD *Fregata ariel*   Rare tropical vagrant

76 cm, 1000 g. Diagnostic *thin white tab extends from the chest onto the armpits and base of the underwing*. Adult male is otherwise *all dark*. Adult female has white of chest and flanks extending to hindneck as *a white collar* contrasting with the *dark hood, chin and throat*. Juvenile has a white chest and gingery head, blotched white when worn. **Habitat:** Tropical seas.

GREATER FRIGATEBIRD *Fregata minor*   Rare tropical vagrant

95 cm, 1500 g. Largest frigatebird. Adult male *all dark*. Adult female and juveniles have white of chest and flanks *extending up to chin and throat* and *not* onto underwing. Juveniles have a gingery head, blotched white when worn. **Habitat:** Tropical seas.

RED-TAILED TROPICBIRD

WHITE-TAILED TROPICBIRD

juv

juv

imm

♂

♀

LESSER FRIGATEBIRD

imm

♂

♀

GREATER FRIGATEBIRD

Plate 22

GANNETS and BOOBIES

Large mainly black and white or brown and white seabirds. Streamlined body with long narrow wings and a long tapering tail. Conical bill, bare facial skin; fully webbed feet. Sexes alike. Juveniles and immatures darker than adults, taking several years to attain full adult plumage. Flight steady and direct; short periods of deliberate flapping and long glides. Feed on fish and squid caught by spectacularly diving into the sea, often from a considerable height. Often sit on the surface between feeding bouts. Gannets favour temperate and subtropical seas, whereas boobies favour tropical and subtropical seas. Gannets nest on the ground in large dense colonies; boobies nest on the ground or in trees singly or in loose colonies. Lay 1–4 plain pale eggs.

AUSTRALASIAN GANNET (Takapu)   *Morus serrator*   Common native

89 cm, 2.3 kg. *White with buff-yellow head and most flight feathers black* (but not the three innermost secondaries or tertials as in Masked Booby); amount of black in the tail varies with age and moult, adults typically have only 4 central feathers black. Bill pale bluish grey; feet slate grey with blue-yellow lines on legs and toes. Juvenile is grey-brown spotted above, white with brown streaks below, and a dark bill. Adult plumage is attained over 3–5 years, head and underparts whitening first, whereas the rump and tail often remains blotched. **Habitat:** Breeds on many islands and some headlands around the NZ coast. Feeds mostly in coastal waters over the continental shelf. Most juveniles move to the seas off eastern and southern Australia and return when 3–7 years old. **Breeding:** Jul–Jan.

MASKED BOOBY   *Sula dactylatra*   Locally uncommon native

80 cm, 1700 g. Adult resembles adult Australasian Gannet but has *white head, orange-yellow or pink bill, black face mask* with yellow eye. Black trailing edge of upperwing includes tertials and so extends to body; tail all dark. Feet purplish grey. Juvenile has mottled brown upperwings, paler back, heavily streaked (almost brown) head and neck grading to white on the collar and lower neck, and a pale yellowish bill. **Habitat:** Tropical and subtropical seas; in NZ region, breeds at Kermadecs. **Breeding:** Aug–Apr.

BROWN BOOBY   *Sula leucogaster*   Rare tropical vagrant

70 cm, 1200 g. *Dark chocolate brown, sharply cut off at mid-breast from white undersurface of body*; centre of underwing white. Legs yellow or greenish yellow. Male has blue facial skin and yellowish-grey bill; female has yellow facial skin and base of bill. Juvenile like adult, but brown parts paler, white parts mottled grey-brown, and less white on underwing. Bill and facial skin blue-grey; legs flesh-grey. **Habitat:** Tropical seas.

AUSTRALASIAN GANNET

juv

juv

imm

MASKED BOOBY

juv

juv

BROWN BOOBY

juv

juv

Plate 23

SHAGS and DARTER

Shags are medium to large aquatic birds. Most are all black, or black above and white below. Bill long, strongly hooked at the tip. Upright posture when perched. Short legs; feet are fully webbed. Many have brightly coloured facial skin when breeding. Sexes alike. In flight, wings short and broad, and neck is extended. Swim with head held uptilted and body low in the water.

BLACK SHAG (Kawau, Great Cormorant) *Phalacrocorax carbo*   Common native

88 cm, 2.2 kg. Largest shag. Black with browner wings and tail, and white patch on cheeks and throat. Facial skin yellow, but early in breeding season it becomes orange-red below eye. Breeding adult also has a white thigh patch, a small black crest on nape and upper neck, and thin white streaks (filoplumes) on the crown and upper neck. Bill grey; eye green; feet black. Immature similar but dull brown above, brown mottled white below, and no throat patch. **Habitat:** Rivers, streams and lakes, also estuaries, harbours and sheltered coastal waters. **Breeding:** Apr–Jan.

PIED SHAG (Karuhiruhi) *Phalacrocorax varius*   Locally common native

81 cm, 2 kg. Large. Glossy black above, face from above eye and all underparts white, except for black thighs. Long grey bill; bare skin buff in front of green eye, pink below bill; eye-ring blue; feet black. Immature similar but brownish above, white underparts streaked and mottled brown. **Habitat:** Coastal, ranging inland only to coastal lagoons and lakes. **Breeding:** All year.

LITTLE BLACK SHAG *Phalacrocorax sulcirostris*   Locally common native

61 cm, 800 g. Small elegant shag. Wholly black with green gloss, *dark-edged feathers give a scalloped effect on back. Long, slender lead-grey bill*; dark facial skin; eye green; feet black. Immature similar but brownish. *Tail short* compared with that of Little Shag. *Gregarious*, often feeding as a co-ordinated pack and flying in V-formation low to the water. **Habitat:** Lakes, estuaries and harbours. Common in North I but rare in South I. **Breeding:** Nov–Apr.

LITTLE SHAG (Kawaupaka) *Phalacrocorax melanoleucos*   Common native

56 cm, 700 g. Smallest shag. Highly variable plumages from all black to pied, but *all have short stubby bills*, yellow in adults, dark in juveniles; eye brown; feet black. Adults have yellow facial skin and small black crest on forehead. *Tail long* compared with that of Little Black Shag. Usually feed solitarily or in small loose groups, but gregarious when roosting and nesting. **Habitat:** Lakes, farm ponds, rivers and streams, also estuaries, harbours and sheltered coastal waters. **Breeding:** Aug–May.

Darters are rather like slim, long-necked shags. When swimming, only their head and neck are visible. They spend long periods perched, mostly in trees, with wings and tail spread.

DARTER *Anhinga melanogaster*   Rare Australian vagrant

90 cm, 1750 g. Large but slim, *very long thin neck, straight dagger-like yellow bill* and very long tail. A white stripe runs from below eye down side of *strongly kinked neck*; prominent *cream streaks on upper wings and long scapular feathers*. Male otherwise all brownish black except for red patch on foreneck. Female and immatures paler with upperparts grey-brown and underparts white or pale buff. In flight, long broad wings and kinked neck; rapid shallow wingbeats interspersed with glides. **Habitat:** Lakes, coastal lagoons and estuaries.

BLACK SHAG

juv

breeding

PIED SHAG

juv

DARTER

♂

♀

LITTLE BLACK SHAG

juv

white-throated phase

pied phase

intermediate phase

juv

LITTLE SHAG

Plate 24

SHAGS

SPOTTED SHAG (Parekareka)   *Stictocarbo punctatus*   **Locally common endemic**

70 cm, 1200 g. Slender *grey* shag with *yellow* feet and long slender brown bill. Breeding adult has small black spots on back and wings; rump, tail and thighs black; underparts grey; *a broad white stripe from above eye down sides of the neck*, and sparse white streaks (filoplumes) on neck and thighs; conspicuous double crest, curled forward; green facial skin. Non-breeding adult lacks crests and has obscure white stripe on neck, yellow facial skin, and paler underparts. Immature is paler and browner, lacks distinct head or neck markings. In flight, looks very slender and pale with darker rump and tail. Flies low to the water, often in strings, with rapid wingbeats. **Habitat:** Estuaries, harbours and coastal waters around mainland NZ. **Breeding:** All year.

PITT ISLAND SHAG   *Stictocarbo featherstoni*   **Locally common endemic**

63 cm, 1200 g. Like Spotted Shag but darker, no white neck stripe and facial skin apple green in breeding season. **Habitat:** Coastal waters around Chatham Is only. **Breeding:** Aug–Mar.

KING SHAG   *Leucocarbo carunculatus*   **Rare endemic**

76 cm, 2.5 kg. Large black and white shag with *pink* feet. White patches on wings appear as a *white bar on the folded wing*; yellow-orange fleshy swellings (caruncles) above base of bill; other facial skin and throat (gular) pouch reddish in breeding season, otherwise grey-blue; eye-ring blue. **Habitat:** Coastal waters of Marlborough Sounds only. **Breeding:** May–Nov.

STEWART ISLAND SHAG   *Leucocarbo chalconotus*   **Locally common endemic**

68 cm, 2.5 kg. Large *pink-footed* shag with pied and bronze phases and some intermediates. Pied phase is like King Shag, but caruncles orange and facial skin purplish; juvenile is brown above and white below, and usually lacks white patches on wings and back. Adult bronze phase is all brownish black with green and blue sheen, orange caruncles and purplish facial skin; juvenile is brown except for some white streaks on breast. Breeding birds develop long black crest on forehead and scattered faint white streaks (filoplumes) on head. **Habitat:** Coastal waters off southeastern South I and Stewart I. **Breeding:** Aug–Mar.

CAMPBELL ISLAND SHAG   *Leucocarbo campbelli*   **Locally common endemic**

63 cm, 2 kg. Like King Shag, but caruncles absent and entire head and neck black, apart from a white chin. **Habitat:** Coastal and offshore waters around Campbell I only. **Breeding:** Nov–May.

AUCKLAND ISLAND SHAG   *Leucocarbo colensoi*   **Locally common endemic**

63 cm, 2 kg. Like King Shag, but caruncles absent. **Habitat:** Coastal and offshore waters around Auckland Is only. **Breeding:** Nov–May.

BOUNTY ISLAND SHAG   *Leucocarbo ranfurlyi*   **Locally common endemic**

71 cm, 2.5 kg. Like King Shag, but caruncles absent. **Habitat:** Coastal and offshore waters around Bounty Is only. **Breeding:** Oct–Mar.

CHATHAM ISLAND SHAG   *Leucocarbo onslowi*   **Locally common endemic**

63 cm, 2.25 kg. Like King Shag, but orange caruncles are large and prominent. **Habitat:** Coastal and offshore waters around the Chatham Is only. **Breeding:** Aug–Mar.

SPOTTED SHAG

imm

PITT ISLAND SHAG

non-breeding

breeding

non-breeding

STEWART ISLAND SHAG

KING SHAG

juv

bronze phase

pied phase

juv pied phase

CHATHAM ISLAND
SHAG

CAMPBELL ISLAND
SHAG

AUCKLAND
ISLAND
SHAG

BOUNTY
ISLAND
SHAG

Plate 25   # HERONS and EGRETS

Medium to large elegant wading birds with long neck and legs, straight dagger-like bill and long unwebbed toes. Flight strong, typically with heavy languid wingbeats on broad wings, neck folded back and head tucked in, and legs trailing. Sexes alike. Immatures of most species are like adults but duller. Many species have ornamental plumes, which may be on the head, back and chest, sometimes distinctively coloured. The colours of bill, facial skin, legs and feet may become brighter or change as birds come into breeding condition. They feed in shallow water or on damp pasture, walking slowly or standing motionless and lunging at prey. Diet is mainly aquatic animals. All may make a harsh grating call in flight; otherwise silent except at breeding colonies. Many species breed and roost communally, others are solitary. Lay 2–5 blue-green eggs on a platform of sticks built in trees or on cliffs.

REEF HERON   *Egretta sacra*   Rare Pacific vagrant

66 cm, 400 g. White phase is stocky with *short legs and long heavy brownish-yellow bill*. Legs yellowish green to grey. In breeding season, strap-like plumes form on nape, chest and back. Feeding stance typically hunched and horizontal. **Habitat:** Coasts. All NZ resident birds are dark (see Plate 26), but a vagrant or colour variation has been seen once in NZ: Canterbury, June 1987.

INTERMEDIATE EGRET   *Egretta intermedia*   Rare Australian vagrant

64 cm, 400 g. All-white heron, smaller than White Heron, larger than Little Egret, and stockier than both. Fully stretched *neck about same length as body* and thicker than White Heron's. *Black line of gape ends level with eye*. In breeding plumage, extensive filamentous *plumes on back and chest*. Legs and bill reddish; facial skin green. In non-breeding, bill and facial skin yellow; legs black, paler grey above 'knees'. **Habitat:** Freshwater and coastal wetlands, occasionally pasture.

WHITE HERON (Kotuku)   *Egretta alba*   Uncommon native

92 cm, 900 g. Clearly the largest all-white heron. Long thin S-shaped neck with a distinct kink one-third back from the head; fully stretched *neck is longer than the body*; *black line of gape extends past the eye*. In breeding plumage, elegant filamentous *plumes on back* extend beyond the folded wings and the tail. Bill black; facial skin green; legs black, yellowish above 'knees'. In non-breeding, plumes absent, bill yellow, facial skin greenish yellow and legs black. Usually solitary, standing or walking sedately in shallow water. **Habitat:** Coastal freshwater wetlands and estuaries, occasionally wet pasture. In NZ, breeds only at Okarito, West Coast, but disperses throughout mainland. **Breeding:** Sep–Jan.

LITTLE EGRET   *Egretta garzetta*   Uncommon Australian migrant

60 cm, 300 g. Small *dainty* all-white heron with *long slender black bill*; facial skin yellow; legs and feet black except for *yellow soles*. *Black line of gape ends level with eye*. In breeding season, plumes on *nape, chest and back*; the 2 nape plumes are strap-like, whereas chest and back plumes are filamentous. *Very active when feeding*, dashing about in pursuit of fish, often with wings raised and with a high-stepping gait. Often solitary but may associate with White Herons. **Habitat:** Coastal lakes and estuaries.

CATTLE EGRET   *Bubulcus ibis*   Locally common Australian migrant

50 cm, 360 g. *Small stocky and short-necked* (shorter than body) heron with *yellow bill*, grey legs and feet, and a *heavy jowl* of feathers under the bill. In breeding plumage, orange-buff plumes on head, neck and breast. Transitional stages from all white to buff common from September onwards. Non-breeding and immature birds all white but can have a faint buff wash on the crown. **Habitat:** *Usually associate with farm animals, especially cattle*, in damp pasture. May return to the same farms or group of farms for autumn and winter year after year.

REEF HERON
white phase

INTERMEDIATE EGRET

breeding

WHITE HERON

non-breeding

breeding

LITTLE EGRET

CATTLE EGRET

breeding

breeding

Plate 26   HERONS, EGRETS and BITTERNS

WHITE-FACED HERON   *Ardea novaehollandiae*   **Abundant native**

67 cm, 550 g. Slim *bluish-grey heron with white face, chin and upper throat*; bill black, legs greenish yellow. Strap-shaped plumes, more prominent in the breeding season, are long and pale grey on the back and short and pinkish brown on the chest. Juvenile like adult but lacks plumes and the white face is reduced, often white chin only. Flight slow, often high, with steady beats of 2-toned wings. **Habitat:** Occupies a wide variety of habitats from coastal estuaries and lagoons to rivers, lakes and farmland. Nests in solitary pairs high in trees, especially eucalypts and shelterbelt pines on farmland. **Breeding:** Jun–Feb.

REEF HERON (Matuku moana)   *Egretta sacra*   **Uncommon native**

66 cm, 400 g. Dark phase uniformly *slaty-grey* heron with a long *heavy horn-coloured-to-yellowish bill*; legs relatively short, yellow-green. Early in breeding season, long strap-like plumes form on back and short ones form on nape and foreneck. Juvenile browner and lacks plumes. *Feeding stance hunched and almost horizontal*; flight slow just above the water surface. Usually solitary or in pairs. **Habitat:** Mangrove inlets, rocky shores, wave platforms and sometimes on intertidal mudflats. Commonest in Northland, decreasing southward and uncommon in South, Stewart and Chatham Is. **Breeding:** Sep–Mar.

Bitterns are specialised for living in swamps; typically short-necked and camouflaged brown with dark and pale streaks, especially on underparts. Sexes alike. When disturbed, they 'freeze', with body and bill pointing skywards, sometimes swaying with raupo or reeds moving in the breeze.

AUSTRALASIAN BITTERN (Matuku)   *Botaurus poiciloptilus*   **Rare native**

71 cm; ♂ 1400 g, ♀ 1000 g. *Large bulky thick-necked bittern, mottled brown and buff.* Secretive, partially nocturnal, generally keeping within dense cover where its plumage blends with the vegetation. When flushed, rises with broad rounded wings labouring. Flight direct, neck withdrawn, legs trailing and with slow steady wing-beats. Usually solitary. During breeding, distinctive *deep booming calls*, like air being blown over an open bottle. **Habitat:** Mainly freshwater wetlands, especially with dense cover of raupo or reeds. Some movement to coastal wetlands in autumn and winter. **Breeding:** Sep–Feb.

LITTLE BITTERN   *Ixobrychus minutus*   **Rare Australian vagrant**

30 cm, 85 g. *Very small bittern.* Adult male has *large buff wing patches* contrasting with black flight feathers, back and tail; ginger sides to face and neck. Adult female like male, but black replaced with brown. Juvenile yellowish buff, heavily streaked dark brown. Flight as in Australasian Bittern; adults show *prominent pale patches on dark upperwings*. **Habitat:** Freshwater wetlands. One NZ record: Westport, February 1987.

WHITE-FACED HERON

juv

REEF HERON

juv

AUSTRALASIAN BITTERN

♂ ♀ juv ♀

LITTLE BITTERN

Plate 27

CRANES, PELICANS and HERONS

Cranes are tall elegant birds with a stout straight bill, longer than the head. The inner secondary flight feathers form plumes that overhang the tail, like a 'bustle'. Sexes alike. They often soar in thermals.

BROLGA   *Grus rubicundus* **Rare Australian vagrant**

115 cm; ♂ 7 kg, ♀ 5 kg. *Very tall stately grey crane* with *scarlet head and nape*, except for grey crown and ear coverts; eye yellow. Juvenile has pink face and crown. In flight, shallow wingbeats, *neck and legs extended*, grey wings with black primaries. **Habitat:** Swampy margins of lakes and ponds, and damp pasture.

Pelicans are large bulky birds with an enormous bill and gular (throat) pouch. Short legs make them ungainly on land, but they swim gracefully. Fly strongly with head tucked in, often in a flock in V formation, or soar high on thermals. They feed mainly on fish scooped from the water, often feeding in a group to surround a shoal of fish. Favour large open waterbodies.

AUSTRALIAN PELICAN   *Pelecanus conspicillatus* **Rare Australian vagrant**

170 cm, 5 kg. *Enormous white bird with huge pink bill and pouch*; upperwing black with a large white panel; underwing white with black primaries. Juvenile brown where adult black. **Habitat:** Occasionally recorded in freshwater and tidal wetlands in NZ.

WHITE-NECKED HERON   *Ardea pacifica* **Rare Australian vagrant**

90 cm, 900 g. Robust *dark grey heron with a white head, neck and upper breast*; variable line of dark spots down the front of the neck. Greenish sheen and maroon plumes on back are prominent in the breeding season. Juvenile lacks plumes and is more heavily spotted and barred brown on neck and breast. In flight, upperparts dark with a striking *white patch at the bend of the wing*. **Habitat:** Margins of swamps, ponds and dams, and damp pasture.

NANKEEN NIGHT HERON   *Nycticorax caledonicus* **Rare native**

57 cm, 800 g. *Stocky rounded short-necked heron, rufous brown or heavily streaked and spotted brown.* Thick black bill; short yellow legs. Adult has rufous-brown (nankeen) upperparts, paler underparts, black cap. When breeding, 2 long slender white plumes hang from the nape. Juvenile dark brown, heavily spotted and streaked pale buff. In flight, looks heavy-headed, round-winged and short-tailed, and has shallower and faster wingbeats than other herons. Usually feeds at dusk or night and roosts in trees by day. **Habitat:** Margins of freshwater wetlands or tidal lagoons. Vagrant until it started breeding on Whanganui River in 1990s. **Breeding:** Season unknown in NZ.

BROLGA

AUSTRALIAN PELICAN

WHITE-NECKED HERON

NANKEEN NIGHT HERON

juv

Plate 28

SPOONBILLS and IBISES

Large heron-like waterbirds with flat spoon-shaped bill (spoonbills) or strongly downcurved bill (ibises). Sexes alike. They fly with neck outstretched, rapid wingbeats alternating with long glides. Roost in trees; breed in colonies with platform nests made from twigs and tidal debris. Disperse widely after breeding. Silent away from colonies. Diet is fish, crustaceans and other aquatic invertebrates.

ROYAL SPOONBILL *Platalea regia* Locally common native

77 cm, 1700 g. *Large brilliantly white bird with long black spoon-shaped bill* and black legs. Adult has black facial skin marked with a yellow patch above each eye and a red spot in the centre of the forehead, and the surface of the bill is wrinkled. In breeding plumage, large white drooping plumes on the rear of the head and a yellowish wash across breast. Juvenile has plain black facial skin, smooth bill and small black tips to wings. Feeds by walking slowly forwards in shallow water, *sweeping partly open bill from side to side*. **Habitat:** Tidal mudflats, occasionally on margins of freshwater lakes. Main breeding colonies at Okarito, Vernon Lagoons (Marlborough), islands just off Otago, and Invercargill Estuary. **Breeding:** Sep–Feb.

YELLOW-BILLED SPOONBILL *Platalea flavipes* Rare Australian vagrant

88 cm, 1900 g. Like Royal Spoonbill, but plumage off-white and *bill and legs pale yellow*. Facial skin pale grey, bordered by a black line. In breeding plumage, medium-length stiff white plumes on lower neck, thin black lace-like plumes on wings, and red patches in front of eye. Feeds by sweeping partly open bill from side to side in shallow water. **Habitat:** Mainly inland wetlands and wet pasture.

GLOSSY IBIS *Plegadis falcinellus* Uncommon Australian vagrant

60 cm, 500 g. Slender *glossy dark brown ibis with long downcurved bill*. At a distance, stance like a feeding Pukeko. In breeding plumage, head, neck and upperparts deep glossy reddish brown, wings iridescent green; bill and facial skin grey, bordered at the base with a conspicuous white line. Non-breeding and juvenile dull brown with variable white mottling on head and neck. Flies with head and neck outstretched like a shag, but alternates rapid wingbeats with short glides. Feeds mainly by probing in soft mud. **Habitat:** Margins of freshwater lakes and swamps, and damp pasture. Occasional irruptions into NZ.

AUSTRALIAN WHITE IBIS *Threskiornis molucca* Rare Australian vagrant

70 cm, 2 kg. Large scruffy *white ibis with long heavy downcurved bill and unfeathered black head*. In breeding plumage, short yellowish plumes on foreneck, and long frilly black tertials droop over tail and folded wing. Non-breeding lacks neck plumes, and tertials shorter and greyer. Juvenile has head and neck fully feathered dark grey and white. In flight, neck outstretched, wings tipped black, and in adults a line of red bare skin shows on the underwing. Walks slowly, probing in mud. **Habitat:** Freshwater or brackish wetlands and wet pasture.

breeding

juv

ROYAL SPOONBILL

non-breeding

YELLOW-BILLED SPOONBILL

GLOSSY IBIS

breeding

non-breeding

AUSTRALIAN WHITE IBIS

Plate 29 **WATERFOWL**

Aquatic birds with a small rounded head, short flattened bill, rounded body, short legs, webbed feet and a waddling gait on land. They fly strongly with neck outstretched. Sexes alike in swans and geese, but male ducks are usually more colourful than females. Lay large clutches. Chicks leave the nest within days but are guarded for several months until they can fly.

BLACK SWAN *Cygnus atratus* — Common Australian introduction

120 cm; ♂ 6 kg, ♀ 5 kg. *Very large black swan*. Bill crimson with white tip and bar near tip. Juvenile is ashy brown with a dull red bill. Takes off laboriously and noisily, running across the surface, wings striking on each downstroke. Flies with long neck extended and slow deep wingbeats, showing *prominent white wing tips*. Flocks fly in long skeins. *Voice a musical bugling*. Feeds mainly on vegetation by dabbling at the surface, upending to reach bottom plants, or grazing on nearby damp pasture. **Habitat:** Lakes, estuaries and parks; sometimes seen at sea or on pasture. **Breeding:** Jul–Feb.

MUTE SWAN *Cygnus olor* — Rare European introduction

150 cm; ♂ 12 kg, ♀ 10 kg. *Very large white swan*. Bill orange with a black knob at the base, larger in breeding males. Juvenile grey-brown, paler than juvenile Black Swan; grey bill bordered with black at the base and lacking knob. Not mute but usually silent. Noisy 'swishing' flight with long neck extended. **Habitat:** Lakes, parks and private waterfowl collections. **Breeding:** Sep–Jan.

CANADA GOOSE *Branta canadensis* — Common North American introduction

83 cm; ♂ 5.4 kg, ♀ 4.5 kg. *Large brown goose* with pale brown and white barring below; *black neck and head with conspicuous white patch on cheeks and chin*. Loud *honking* call given when alarmed and in flight. Flocks fly in V formation. Grazes on pasture, young crops and aquatic plants. **Habitat:** High-country pasture, freshwater lakes and margins, and coastal lagoons. **Breeding:** Sep–Dec.

CAPE BARREN GOOSE *Cereopsis novaehollandiae* — Rare Australian introduction

87 cm, 5 kg. *Large bulky pale grey goose* with dark spots on scapulars and wing coverts. *Bill short and largely covered by a greenish-yellow cere*; legs pink and feet black. In flight, uniformly grey with black tail and wingtips. Grazes on pasture plants. **Habitat:** Parks, occasionally on lakes. Vagrants may occasionally reach NZ.

FERAL GOOSE *Anser anser* — Common European introduction

80 cm, 3 kg. The familiar domestic goose of farms and parks, often feral. Males are all white, females white with brown on wings and thighs. Juveniles all grey-brown. Bill, legs and feet orange-pink. Usually graze away from water. **Habitat:** Lakes, estuaries and farmland.

juv

LACK SWAN

juv

MUTE SWAN

CANADA GOOSE

CAPE BARREN GOOSE

♂

♀

FERAL GOOSE

Plate 30 **WATERFOWL**

PARADISE SHELDUCK (Putangitangi)   *Tadorna variegata*   Common endemic

63 cm; ♂ 1700 g, ♀ 1400 g. Large goose-like duck with *orange-chestnut undertail* and tertials. Male has *black head with greenish gloss, body dark grey finely barred black*. Female has *brilliant white head, body bright orange-chestnut*, obscured by darker fine barring in eclipse plumage. Juveniles like male, but immature females develop white patches around eyes and at base of bill. In flight, prominent white patches on upperwings. Often call; male a deep 'zonk-zonk . . .', female a shrill 'zeek, zeek . . .' Mostly seen as pairs or in large flocks, especially during the moult in Dec–Mar. **Habitat:** Farmland, lakes, ponds and high-country riverbeds. **Breeding:** Aug–Dec.

CHESTNUT-BREASTED SHELDUCK   *Tadorna tadornoides*   Rare native

65 cm; ♂ 1600 g, ♀ 1300 g. Like male Paradise Shelduck, but *undertail black and chest and lower neck orange-chestnut, bordered above by thin white collar*. Male has upper back and breast pale orange-chestnut, thin white collar, and occasionally has a small white patch at base of bill. Female has darker orange-chestnut upper back and breast, very thin white collar and white patches at base of bill and around eye. Juvenile like female but smaller, duller and lacks collar. Often seen with Paradise Shelduck in NZ. **Habitat:** Freshwater and brackish lakes. First recorded in 1973 and have bred at least twice in eastern South I. **Breeding:** Season unknown in NZ.

BLUE DUCK (Whio)   *Hymenolaimus malacorhynchos*   Uncommon endemic

53 cm; ♂ 900 g, ♀ 750 g. *Blue-grey duck with a pale pink bill*, tipped with black flaps. Adult has yellow eyes, breast spotted reddish chestnut. Sexes similar. Juvenile has dull grey bill and eyes, and fewer breast spots. Uniformly grey in flight. Male call a whistling 'whio, whio' (fee-o, fee-o); female call a rattling growl; often call together in flight. Remain in territorial pairs all year. Seen standing on rocks or feeding with head and neck underwater. **Habitat:** Fast-flowing mountain streams and rivers, mainly in native forest or tussock grassland, occasionally on lakes. **Breeding:** Jul–Jan.

AUSTRALIAN WOOD DUCK   *Chenonetta jubata*   Rare Australian vagrant

48 cm, 800 g. Pale grey duck with chest spotted brown, head dark brown, and short thin bill. Male has dark brown head and neck, with a short black mane on back of head; grey flanks. Female has pale lines above and below eye; flanks broadly barred brown and white. Juvenile like female but duller. In the water, sits higher than other ducks. Spends much time out of water grazing or roosting. Upright stance. Call a rising 'mew' or 'wee-ow'. **Habitat:** Grassland near wetlands.

GRASS (Plumed) WHISTLING DUCK   *Dendrocygna eytoni*   Rare Australian vagrant

50 cm, 800 g. Pale brown duck with goose-like profile and *stiff cream plumes curving up from the flanks to above back*. Bill flecked pink and grey. Sexes alike. Juvenile paler with small plumes. In flight, head held below the horizontal, back hunched and legs trailing. When flying, constantly twittering and whistling; the wings also whistle. **Habitat:** Grassland near wetlands.

PARADISE SHELDUCK

♀

♂

♂

♀

♀ imm

♀ eclipse

CHESTNUT-BREASTED SHELDUCK

♂

♀

♀

BLUE DUCK

AUSTRALIAN WOOD DUCK

GRASS WHISTLING DUCK

MALLARD   *Anas platyrhynchos*   **Abundant European introduction**

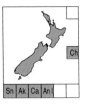

58 cm; ♂ 1300 g, ♀ 1100 g. The familiar duck of parks and farm ponds. *All have orange legs and feet, and a blue speculum bordered with thin black and broader white bands front and back.* Breeding male has dark glossy green head, chestnut breast, pale grey body, black rump and undertail; bill yellow-green. Female is streaked and spotted brown and buff on body and wings; bill brownish grey with orange at base, sides and tip. Eclipse male like female but has greyer head and neck, with remnants of green on crown and nape, and chestnut wash on breast. Juvenile similar to female. Variable plumage because of interbreeding with Grey Duck. Feeds by dabbling on water surface or by upending; also grazes and eats cereals. Rises nearly vertically from water and flies with fast shallow wingbeats. Female call the well-known 'quack, quack'; male call a soft high-pitched 'quek'. **Habitat:** Wetlands, estuaries, rivers, farm ditches, parks and cereal crops. **Breeding:** Jul–Jan.

GREY DUCK (Parera)   *Anas superciliosa*   **Common native**

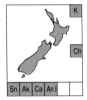

55 cm; ♂ 1100 g, ♀ 1000 g. Like female Mallard but *darker with conspicuously striped pale head, grey bill, greenish-brown legs and feet. Green speculum with black borders and thin white band on trailing edge only.* Sexes alike. In flight, looks dark with a very pale head and upper neck. Calls like Mallard. Has interbred extensively with the Mallard to produce paler birds with less distinct facial stripes and greyish bills, yellowish-brown legs and feet, and blue speculum. **Habitat:** Pure birds mainly in remote wetlands, including forest lakes and rivers; uncommon in agricultural and urban habitats dominated by Mallards. **Breeding:** Aug–Jan.

AUSTRALASIAN SHOVELER (Kuruwhengi)   *Anas rhynchotis*   **Common native**

49 cm; ♂ 650 g, ♀ 600 g. Duck with heavy spatulate bill. Sits low in the water and profile shows no apparent forehead. Breeding male has *blue-grey head with a white crescent in front of golden eye*; breast off-white with extensive dark brown mottling; flanks bright chestnut with prominent *white patch at base of tail*. Bill dark grey; legs orange. Eclipse male has head speckled blue-grey, underparts mottled bronzy chestnut, with paler (sometimes almost white) breast, and lacks white flank patch. Female streaked and spotted brown and buff on body; bill grey with some pale orange at base and sides in some birds. In flight, *upperwing has sky-blue panel on inner forewing, narrow white wingbars and dark green speculum.* Flight swift, wings noticeably narrow and pointed. Whistling wings and jinking flight as it approaches to land. Birds utter a quiet 'cuck-cuck-cuck . . .' Feeds by sieving seeds and small aquatic animals through immersed bill. **Habitat:** Mainly shallow lowland wetlands, and muddy estuaries. **Breeding:** Oct–Feb.

NORTHERN SHOVELER   *Anas clypeata*   **Rare Arctic vagrant**

50 cm, 650 g. Like Australasian Shoveler, including the same profile and upperwing pattern, but male in breeding plumage has *pure dark green head, and clean white breast extends to shoulders.* Eclipse male can have crescent on face, but head greener and flanks and undertail paler than Australasian Shoveler. Female paler and greyer than Australasian Shoveler, and usually has more orange on sides of bill and more white on outer tail. **Habitat:** Lowland wetlands.

PINK-EARED DUCK   *Malacorhynchus membranaceus*   **Rare Australian vagrant**

40 cm, 400 g. Small duck with a large square-ended bill, black flaps at the tip. Back and wings grey-brown, distinctly *striped dark brown and white on lower neck, breast and flanks*; white flank patch extends across rump; undertail yellow-brown. *Large dark patch around eye,* contrasting white eye-ring, and small pink patch on ear coverts. In flight, *white rump contrasts with grey-brown upperwing and back, and dark brown white-tipped tail.* Constant chirruping call on the water and in flight. Feeds by filtering with bill submerged up to eyes. **Habitat:** Lakes. One NZ record: Auckland, June 1990.

MALLARD

♂

♀

♂ eclipse

GREY DUCK

♂ eclipse

♂

♀

AUSTRALASIAN SHOVELER

♂ eclipse

♂

♀

NORTHERN SHOVELER

PINK-EARED DUCK

Plate 32

WATERFOWL

GREY TEAL (Tete) *Anas gracilis* Common native

43 cm; ♂ 525 g, ♀ 425 g. *Delicate light grey-brown duck with pale grey cheeks, chin and foreneck.* Silhouette rounded, including head. Sits high and upright on the water. Bill blue-grey; *eye red*. Sexes alike. Juvenile paler, eye brown. In flight, speculum black with a green sheen, a narrow white bar behind, and a *prominent white triangle* in front; underwing white in the centre. Wingbeats very fast. Feeds by filtering on water surface or dredging bill in soft mud. **Habitat:** Lowland lakes and lagoons, and estuaries. **Breeding:** Jun–Feb.

CHESTNUT TEAL *Anas castanea* Rare Australian vagrant

45 cm, 650 g. Like larger and darker-faced Grey Teal. Breeding male has *dark glossy green head and neck, bright chestnut underparts, a large white flank patch and a black undertail*. Female and juvenile like Grey Teal, but *pale buff rather than whitish chin and throat*, and dark crown is less distinct. Eclipse male like a dark female, but traces of colour are usually apparent. Bill blue-grey; *eye red*. In flight, wing pattern like Grey Teal. **Habitat:** Lowland lakes and estuaries.

BROWN TEAL (Pateke) *Anas aucklandica* Rare endemic

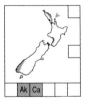

48 cm; ♂ 600 g, ♀ 500 g. Like Chestnut Teal, but *eye brown with narrow white eye-ring* in all plumages. In flight, *lacks white triangle* in front of speculum. Breeding male has a glossy green head, an *indistinct narrow white collar* and a conspicuous white flank patch. Eclipse male, female and juvenile are warm brown; breast is mottled dark brown. Bill blue-black. Auckland I Teal flightless, with more subdued colouring. Campbell I Teal also flightless and with prominent white eye-ring. Gather to roost in flocks by day, and feed at dusk and at night. **Habitat:** Tidal creeks, lagoons and swamps, and adjacent wet pasture. Subantarctic subspecies feed in peaty creeks and soaks, and on coastal platforms and kelp beds. Brown Teal mostly on Great Barrier I and in Northland. **Breeding:** Jun–Nov; Auckland I Teal: Dec–Feb.

WHITE-EYED DUCK *Aythya australis* Rare Australian vagrant

48 cm, 900 g. Diving duck like NZ Scaup, but *chocolate brown with white undertail; forehead slopes gently*. Bill dark grey with whitish band near the end, tipped black. Male has *white eye*; female brown eye. Female and juvenile lighter browner than male, and white patch on bill is smaller. In flight, upperwing has a broad white trailing band *from wingtip to body*; underwing white. Feeds and roosts on water, rarely coming onto land. **Habitat:** Large deep freshwater lakes, occasionally estuaries.

NEW ZEALAND SCAUP (Papango) *Aythya novaeseelandiae* Uncommon endemic

40 cm, 650 g. Small blackish diving duck with *rounded toy 'rubber duckie' profile* and a *steep forehead*. Male *glossy black*, maroon on flanks and brown on belly. Bill blue-grey, tipped black; eye *golden-yellow*. Female *blackish brown*, usually with *vertical white band at the base of the bill*. Bill with faint black tip; eye brown. Juvenile like female but lacks white on face and bill dark grey. In flight, upperwing has a broad white trailing band from wingtip, but *not reaching body*; underwing white. Patters along water when taking off and flies low to the surface. Feeds on bottom weeds and invertebrates by diving. **Habitat:** Large deep freshwater lakes, including hydro lakes; also coastal dune lakes. **Breeding:** Oct–Mar.

GREY TEAL

CHESTNUT TEAL

♀

♂

BROWN TEAL

♀

♂ breeding

WHITE-EYED DUCK

♀

♂

♀

Auckland Island Teal

♂

NEW ZEALAND SCAUP

♂

juv

♀

Plate 33   **RAPTORS**

Diurnal birds of prey with long fingered or pointed wings; long tail; short hooked bill with coloured facial skin at the base of the bill (cere); powerful, largely unfeathered legs with long sharp talons for grasping prey or gripping carrion. Sexes usually alike, but females larger. Juveniles darker than adults.

AUSTRALASIAN HARRIER (Kahu)   *Circus approximans*   Abundant native

♂ 55 cm, 650 g; ♀ 60 cm, 850 g. *Large brown hawk with long fingered wings held in shallow V*, and a long slightly rounded tail. Becomes paler with age. Juvenile very dark brown with a prominent *white patch on back of head*; brown uppertail and brown eye. In adult, head and upperparts dark brown, face paler; *uppertail white*, tail light brown barred dark brown; underparts reddish brown streaked dark brown, underwings barred at tips and on trailing half. Some very old males have frosty-grey upperparts, pale buff underparts and white underwings. Eye yellow in males, very pale yellow in females. Commonly soars and glides in search of prey or carrion; often feeds on road-killed animals. **Habitat:** Farmland, tussockland and swamps, also forest edges. **Breeding:** Sep–Feb.

NEW ZEALAND FALCON (Karearea)   *Falco novaeseelandiae*   Uncommon endemic

♂ 43 cm, 300 g; ♀ 47 cm, 500 g. *Fast-flying raptor with rapid beats of long pointed wings*; also soars and glides. Adult has head, sides of face and vertical patch (like drooping moustache) below eye dark brownish black, faint rufous eyebrow; nape, back, wings and tail bluish black, faintly barred buff. Base of bill and chin white, throat and sides of neck buff streaked dark brown; breast and belly dark brown narrowly barred white; thigh and undertail rufous. Bill black, greyer at base; cere, legs and feet yellow; eye dark brown. Juvenile distinctly darker brown and less boldly marked. Bush Falcon (North and northwestern South Is) as above; eastern form (eastern South I) larger and paler; southern form (southwestern South, Stewart and Auckland Is) intermediate, more rufous on Auckland I. Often perches high in trees or on a rock, swoops to catch prey. Call a loud rapid 'kek-kek-kek'. **Habitat:** Forests and bush patches, open tussockland of South I. Juveniles wander to cities, orchards, riverbeds and offshore islands. **Breeding:** Sep–Feb.

BLACK KITE   *Milvus migrans*   Rare Australian vagrant

♂ 50 cm, 550 g; ♀ 55 cm, 600 g. Large *dark-brown* raptor with paler head and shoulder patches. Soars or glides on long fingered wings held flat, and frequently twists its *long forked tail*. Adult has forehead and chin grey merging into brown on the crown, cheeks and throat; rest of body dark brown with some darker streaks. Pale shoulder patch when bird is at rest. Bill black, cere yellow, legs and feet yellow. Juvenile paler, and head, neck and breast heavily streaked buff; upperwing mottled buff; bill black, cere grey, legs and feet yellow. **Habitat:** Open country.

BLACK FALCON   *Falco subniger*   Rare Australian vagrant

♂ 50 cm, 600 g; ♀ 54 cm, 800 g. Like *large* NZ Falcon but uniformly sooty brown except for pale streaked chin and face, and dark grey glossy wash on underwing and undertail. Juvenile darker with pale feather edges and faint barring under tail and wings. **Habitat:** Open country and scattered forest.

NANKEEN KESTREL   *Falco cenchroides*   Uncommon Australian vagrant

♂ 32 cm, 160 g; ♀ 34 cm, 180 g. Small long-winged and long-tailed raptor with *habit of hovering*, poised in mid-air facing into the wind with tail fanned. In flight, back and upperwings cinnamon brown with black wingtips; underparts white with buff wash on breast and variable fine dark streaks. Male has *blue-grey head* streaked black, and *tail blue-grey* with black band near tip and narrow white tip. Female and juvenile have *pale rufous head*, finely streaked black; *tail pale rufous* with black band near tip and narrow white tip. **Habitat:** Open country.

AUSTRALASIAN HARRIER

juv

ad

juv

ad ♀

ad ♂

imm

NEW ZEALAND
FALCON

ad

juv

BLACK KITE

BLACK FALCON

NANKEEN
KESTREL

♂

♀

♂

Plate 34   **GAMEBIRDS**

All gamebirds are introduced, often with great persistence and cost. Small to large plump birds that feed on the ground. Omnivorous but mainly take plant food, scratching and digging at the ground surface with legs and strong claws, and bill. When disturbed, they crouch, run to cover, or burst from cover with whirring wings and alarm notes, flying fast and low to pitch a short distance away. Sexes usually differ: females and immatures have subdued plumage that blends with the surroundings; males are sometimes brightly coloured, but even strongly patterned males blend with their surroundings. Immatures are usually seen with adults, so identity should not be a problem.

PHEASANT   *Phasianus colchicus*   Common European introduction

♂ 80 cm, 1400 g; ♀ 60 cm, 1200 g. Long-tailed gamebird. Male colourful, mainly rich orange-reds, glossy dark green head, red facial wattles. Female smaller, pale brown heavily mottled dark brown, lacks facial wattles. Male territorial call a loud, abrupt crow: 'kok-kok', with emphasis on the second syllable. Explodes suddenly from undergrowth when disturbed, with noisy wingbeats and rapid calls, and glides back to cover. **Habitat:** Open scrubland, vegetated sand dunes, riverbanks, and agricultural land with plenty of cover. **Breeding:** Jul–Mar.

PEAFOWL   *Pavo cristatus*   Uncommon Asian introduction

90 cm (+ male's 100 cm tail); ♂ 4.5 kg, ♀ 3.5 kg. Peacock distinctive and well known; peahen smaller, brown mottled black and white, and with a pointed tail. The peacock's loud wailing *trumpet-like cry* – 'kay-yaaw' – draws attention. Roosts in trees. **Habitat:** Parks and private gardens, rough agricultural land with good cover in warm, dry districts.

WILD TURKEY   *Meleagris gallopavo*
Locally common North American introduction

♂ 120 cm, 8 kg; ♀ 90 cm, 4 kg. Large black bird with blue and red head; familiar farmyard Turkey. Male black with paler barred wings and tail; beard of long feathers hangs from upper chest; head and neck naked and wrinkled, blue and red. Female smaller and browner, and lacks beard and neck wattles. The familiar territorial gobbling is mainly by males. Seldom flies, except to roost in trees. **Habitat:** Farmland, especially where there is good cover.

TUFTED GUINEAFOWL   *Numida meleagris*   Rare African introduction

60 cm, 1500 g. Large rounded gamebird with a small blue-grey bare head, red wattles, and a bony horn protruding from the crown. Body slate grey thickly spotted white. Sexes alike. Roosts in trees. **Habitat:** Semiferal at many farms and rural homesteads; a few are feral in rough agricultural land in Northland, Waikato, Rotorua and Wanganui.

PHEASANT

♂

♀

PEAFOWL

♂

♀

WILD TURKEY

♀

♂

TUFTED GUINEAFOWL

Plate 35

GAMEBIRDS

GREY PARTRIDGE   *Perdix perdix*

Rare European introduction

30 cm. Medium-sized *grey* partridge, mottled brown on back and barred chestnut on flanks. Male has *orange-brown face and throat and dark horseshoe-shaped patch on breast*. Female has paler face and less distinct patch on breast. Bill and legs blue-grey. In flight, *mottled upperparts and rusty tail*. Flight fast direct and low with rapid whirring wingbeats; when flushed, a covey usually keeps together. Voice is sharp 'kirrik', likened to rusty gate hinges. **Habitat:** Open country with dense cover.

RED-LEGGED PARTRIDGE   *Alectoris rufa*

Rare European introduction

31 cm. Like Chukor in size, plumage, bright red bill and legs, and voice, but has *black necklace higher on throat, streaked black and white* on lower throat and sides of neck; *crown, nape and hindneck brown*. Flank bars are more chestnut than black. Sexes alike. In flight, shows *plain grey-brown back*. **Habitat:** Open country with dense cover, such as riverbeds flanked by willows and gorse.

CHUKOR   *Alectoris chukar*

Locally common Asian introduction

31 cm; ♂ 600 g, ♀ 500 g. Like Red-legged Partridge but has *solid clear-cut black necklace* that crosses *low on the throat; crown, nape and hindneck grey*. Flank bars are more black than chestnut. Sexes alike. In flight, *upperparts plain grey with rusty wash at base of wings* and rusty outer tail feathers. When flushed, a covey usually scatters. Voice a loud 'chuck-chuck-chuck-per-chuck-per-chuck-chuckar-chuckar-chuckar'. **Habitat:** South I hill country, especially rocky hillsides with tussock and sparse scrub. **Breeding:** Sep–Feb.

CALIFORNIA QUAIL   *Callipepla californica*

Common North American introduction

25 cm, 180 g. Small partridge with *forward-curving topknot crest plume*, smaller in female. Male has a black throat bordered by a white band, blue-grey breast and scaly upperparts. Female duller. Male has a loud *3-syllable call:* 'chi-ca-go' or 'where are you?', with emphasis on the second syllable. **Habitat:** Open country with patches of low scrub, riverbeds flanked by willows and gorse. **Breeding:** Sep–Mar.

BROWN QUAIL   *Synoicus ypsilophorus*

Locally common Australian introduction

18 cm, 100 g. *Very small rounded brown quail*. Mottled black and chestnut above; fine wavy bars below. Bill dark, eye reddish, legs yellowish. Sexes alike. Call a plaintive languid 'ker-wee', the second syllable drawn out and with rising inflexion. **Habitat:** Scrub edges in rough farmland; most common in Northland, uncommon further south. **Breeding:** Sep–Feb.

BOBWHITE QUAIL   *Colinus virginianus*

Rare North American introduction

23 cm, 180 g. Small quail with *longitudinal pale chestnut stripes on the flanks*, dark grey bill and yellowish-brown legs. Male has *white face, black cap and line through eye* to join black necklace across throat, trailing down onto breast. Female has yellowish-buff face and brown markings. Male call a whistling 'poor-bob-white', with accent on the last note. **Habitat:** Low scrub with grassy clearings; may persist in South Auckland and northern Hawke's Bay.

GREY
PARTRIDGE

♂

♀

RED-LEGGED
PARTRIDGE

CHUKOR

CALIFORNIA
QUAIL

♂

♀

BROWN QUAIL

BOBWHITE QUAIL

♂

♀

Plate 36

RAILS and CRAKES

Most are secretive birds of wetlands and are rarely seen except when attracted by taped calls. Plumage is usually a pattern of black, white, brown and chestnut. Immatures are duller. Sexes alike. Body is narrow, for slipping through dense vegetation. Long unwebbed toes spread their weight. The short tail flicks as they walk. Bill stout and dagger-like in rails, shorter in crakes. Fly reluctantly when disturbed but are capable of sustained flight, mainly at night.

WEKA *Gallirallus australis*　　　　Locally common endemic

53 cm; ♂ 1000 g, ♀ 700 g. *Flightless. Brown, streaked black.* Sturdy short bill and legs. The 4 subspecies are separated by plumage colour. Rare North I Weka is greyer below and has brown legs; Buff Weka, introduced to Chatham Is, is the palest; Western Weka (Nelson to Fiordland) is noticeably chestnut, except in Fiordland, where a dark form is common; Stewart I Weka is the smallest and also has a dark form, but paler than Western Weka. Sometimes very inquisitive. Walks quietly, flicking leaves aside with bill in search of food. Runs fast, neck outstretched. *Territorial call a loud repeated 'coo-eet', rising in pitch.* **Habitat:** Forests, scrub and open country with good cover. **Breeding:** Aug–Feb.

BANDED RAIL (Moho-pereru) *Rallus philippensis*　　　　Locally common native

30 cm, 170 g. Strikingly marked but secretive. *Upperparts olive brown and black with white spots, and underparts barred black and white.* A chestnut band crosses chest, and a narrower one passes through eye to hindneck; whitish eye stripe, grey chin and throat. Long stout bill, brown. Juvenile less distinctly marked. Can fly well but, when flushed, flies for a short distance with legs dangling. Call a creaky 'swit', heard mostly at dusk and dawn. **Habitat:** Saltmarshes, mangroves and, less often, freshwater swamps; also some offshore islands. **Breeding:** Sep–Mar.

AUCKLAND ISLAND RAIL *Rallus pectoralis*　　　　Locally common native

21 cm, 90 g. Secretive subspecies of Lewin's Rail of Australia and New Guinea. Smaller and darker than Banded Rail. Back, wings and uppertail olive brown streaked black. Crown, sides of head and neck rufous to gingery brown. Throat and bill grey. Flanks and undertail finely barred black and white. Long slim bill, reddish. Legs pale brown. **Habitat:** Dense scrub cover, tussock and herbfields on Adams and Disappointment Is of the Auckland Is only. **Breeding:** Oct–Dec.

SPOTLESS CRAKE (Puweto) *Porzana tabuensis*　　　　Locally common native

20 cm, 45 g. Small dark rail, secretive but responds to taped calls. Head and underparts leaden grey with a bluish sheen, *upperparts plain dark chocolate brown*, undertail black barred white. Bill short, black; eye and eye-ring red; legs reddish. Juvenile lacks sheen, and chin and throat dull white. Varied calls; usually sharp 'pit-pit', a repeated 'book' and a distinctive *rolling 'purrrrrrrr'*, like an alarm clock going off and gradually running down. **Habitat:** Freshwater wetlands with raupo or sedge, especially in the North I; forest on some offshore islands. **Breeding:** Aug–Feb.

MARSH CRAKE (Koitareke) *Porzana pusilla*　　　　Locally common native

18 cm, 40 g. Tiny slim secretive rail. Like a miniature Banded Rail, but upperparts cinnamon brown *streaked* black and white. Sides of head and underparts blue-grey; flanks, abdomen and undertail are black barred white. Bill, legs and feet greenish; eye red. Juvenile barred brown and buff on underparts, pale buff on cheeks and throat. Readily walks on duckweed and other floating vegetation. Call a harsh *'krek'*, like a fingernail being drawn along a comb. **Habitat:** Dense beds of reeds and rushes in freshwater and estuarine wetlands. **Breeding:** Oct–Jan.

Western
dark phase

WEKA

Buff

Western

AUCKLAND ISLAND RAIL

BANDED RAIL

juv

MARSH CRAKE

juv

SPOTLESS CRAKE

Plate 37

SWAMPHENS and COOTS

Birds of marsh and open water. Most are black, brown and purple-blue. Sexes alike. Wings short and broad. The bill extends onto their forehead as a shield, usually with diagnostic colour. Their strong legs and long toes aid walking on floating vegetation. Toes may be lobed (coots) for specialised swimming. They run well, walk with flicking tail, exposing a white undertail, and swim with bobbing head.

TAKAHE (Notornis) *Porphyrio mantelli*   Rare endemic

63 cm, 3 kg. Like an enormous Pukeko. *Flightless.* Colour ranges from iridescent dark blue head, neck and breast and peacock-blue shoulders to olive-green and blue back and wings. *Bill and shield massive, scarlet,* paler toward the tip; legs and feet red; eye brown. Immature duller; bill and shield dark grey. Mainly vegetarian; *leaving behind chewed and abandoned stems of tussock or other grasses* and 8 cm long *sausage-shaped fibrous droppings.* Male and female duet with a loud Weka-like, but *slow and deep, 'coo-eet';* alarm note a *deep resonant 'oomf'.* **Habitat:** Natural range now tussock grassland and beech forest in mountains west of Lake Te Anau. Introduced to rank grassland on Tiritiri Matangi, Kapiti, Mana and Maus Is. **Breeding:** Oct–Jan.

PUKEKO (Purple Swamphen) *Porphyrio porphyrio*   Abundant native

51 cm; ♂ 1050 g, ♀ 850 g. *Deep blue* with black head and upperparts. *Undertail white, flirted with every step.* Bill and shield scarlet; eye red; legs and feet orange-red. Sexes alike. Immature has much brown and buff in the plumage and on bill and legs. Voice a loud unmusical screech. Runs well and swims with tail held high. Clambers about and may perch in scrub and trees. When disturbed in the open, runs to cover or flies, legs dangling, for a short distance. Flies high at night, calling – a loud harsh screech. **Habitat:** Wetlands, estuaries, short damp pasture and parks. Often in extended family groups. **Breeding:** Aug–Mar.

AUSTRALIAN COOT *Fulica atra*   Locally common native

38 cm; ♂ 570 g, ♀ 520 g. *Black with white bill and shield. No white under tail.* Eye red; legs dark grey, *feet lobed.* Immature dark brown-grey, shield small and pinkish grey. Mainly aquatic; swims with head jerking back and forth, *dives* with a short forward jump to pluck submerged aquatic plants, patters across the surface as it labours to take off. Sometimes comes ashore to graze on short grass. Often in flocks. Main call a loud harsh 'krark'. **Habitat:** Small freshwater lakes and shallow bays of larger lakes. **Breeding:** Aug–Mar.

DUSKY MOORHEN *Gallinula tenebrosa*   Rare Australian vagrant

37 cm, 500 g. Like a Coot but wings olive brown, *shield orange-red, bill red with a yellow tip, and undertail dark with white sides*; legs green with red at 'knee' joint. Immature browner; bill varying from greenish yellow to brown. Wings project high above tail when swimming. Common call a loud explosive 'prurk'. **Habitat:** Weedy shallows or edge of reedbeds of freshwater wetlands, sometimes on nearby pasture.

BLACK-TAILED NATIVE-HEN *Gallinula ventralis*   Rare Australian vagrant

35 cm, 400 g. Similar in size and shape to Dusky Moorhen but more *upright stance with tail held cocked.* Olive brown above, slate grey below, with prominent *white pear-shaped spots on the flanks.* Tail and undertail black; tail flicked constantly. *Shield, upper bill and bill tip green, lower bill orange*; eye yellow; legs brick red. **Habitat:** Feeds on dry land near freshwater wetlands.

TAKAHE

PUKEKO

imm

AUSTRALIAN
COOT

imm

imm

DUSKY MOORHEN

BLACK-TAILED NATIVE-HEN

Plate 38

WADERS

A large diverse group of birds of estuaries, coasts, riverbeds and farmland. Most are long-legged and feed in or near shallow water. Bill shape is varied; short and stubby in those (e.g. dotterels) that peck from the surface, but longer in those that feed in shallow water (e.g. stilts), or probe deeply (e.g. godwits). Flight strong and direct. Often form flocks while roosting or flying, but disperse to feed. Many species seen in NZ breed in the Arctic and arrive in September, with remnants of breeding plumage, and depart in March, often in breeding plumage. Most subadults and a few adults spend the southern winter here.

PIED OYSTERCATCHER (Torea) *Haematopus ostralegus* **Abundant native**

46 cm, 550 g. Striking black and white wader with long stout red bill and short stubby pink legs. *Sharp border on lower chest between black upperparts and white underparts*, a *white tab* extends upwards in front of folded wing. In flight, *white wingbar, rump and lower back*. Orange eye-ring. Sexes alike. Immature has browner plumage, dusky-red bill and dull legs. Forms large roosting and feeding flocks. Flight call a loud shrill 'kleep'. **Habitat:** Breeds inland on riverbeds and farmland, mainly in South I. Migrates to estuaries for autumn and winter. **Breeding:** Aug–Jan.

CHATHAM ISLAND OYSTERCATCHER *Haematopus chathamensis* **Rare endemic**

48 cm, 600 g. Like pied phase Variable Oystercatcher in having a slightly smudgy border on chest, but *shorter bill and thicker legs and feet*. **Habitat:** Rocky and sandy coasts of Chatham Is. **Breeding:** Oct–Mar.

VARIABLE OYSTERCATCHER (Torea, Toreapango) *Haematopus unicolor*
Uncommon endemic

48 cm, 725 g. Variable plumage, from black to pied, with continuous gradient between. Long robust red bill and short stubby pink legs. Pied phase like Pied Oystercatcher but *larger*, bill heavier, and *smudgy* border on chest; most lack tab in front of folded wing. In flight, white wingbar and rump have smudgy edges, and lower back is black or smudgy. Black phase, commonest south of Taranaki and Gisborne, is pure black. Immature has browner plumage, dusky-red bill and dull legs. Flight call a loud shrill 'kleep'. **Habitat:** Breeds on rocky and sandy coasts, rarely on shores of coastal lakes. Some gather on estuaries in autumn and winter. **Breeding:** Sep–Feb.

SPUR-WINGED PLOVER *Vanellus miles* **Abundant native**

38 cm; ♂ 370 g, ♀ 350 g. Conspicuous *noisy* large plover. Black crown, hindneck and shoulders in front of bend of wing; smooth brown back and wings; white rump and tail tipped black. White underparts; wings have dark trailing edge. *Yellow facial patch, wattles and bill*; legs and feet reddish. Spur on bend of wing usually hidden. Juvenile has small wattles, and feathers on upperparts are narrowly edged black and buff. *Flies with slow deliberate beats* of rounded wings. Call a *loud staccato rattle*: 'kerr-kick-ki-ki-ki'. **Habitat:** Farmland, rough grassland, wetland margins and estuaries. **Breeding:** Jun–Dec.

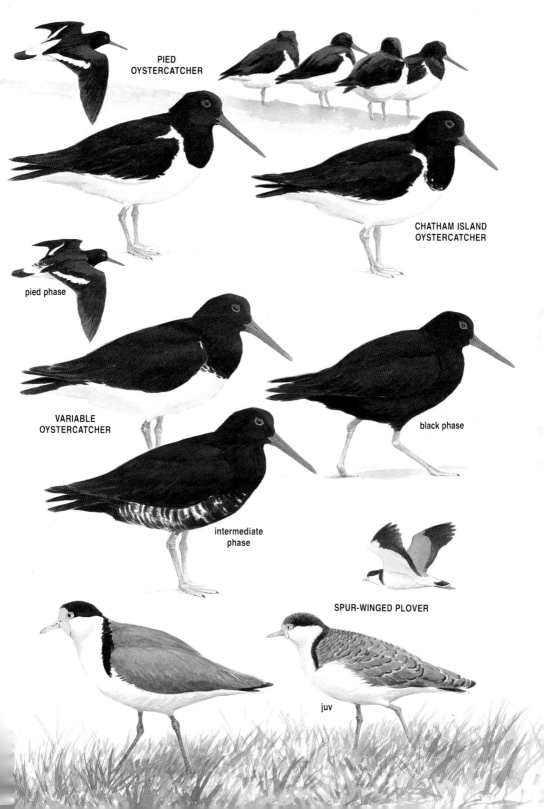

PIED
OYSTERCATCHER

CHATHAM ISLAND
OYSTERCATCHER

pied phase

VARIABLE
OYSTERCATCHER

black phase

intermediate
phase

SPUR-WINGED PLOVER

juv

Plate 39

WADERS

PIED STILT (Poaka) *Himantopus himantopus*

Common native

35 cm, 190 g. Distinctive black and white wader with *extremely long pinkish-red legs* and *long fine black bill*. Variable black on crown, nape, hindneck and collar on the lower neck; black wings and back; grey wash at end of tail. Face, throat and underparts white. Eye red. Juvenile has grey wash on head and neck, dull pink legs, dark brown back and wings. Distinctive *yapping calls*, often heard at night or when breeding birds are disturbed. Hybridises naturally with Black Stilt; intermediate forms not uncommon. **Habitat:** Breeds on riverbeds, lake margins and damp pasture. Form flocks at estuaries and lakes outside breeding season. Many South I and southern North I birds migrate to northern North I after breeding season. **Breeding:** Jul–Jan.

BLACK STILT (Kaki) *Himantopus novaezelandiae*

Rare endemic

40 cm, 220 g. Pure adults *entirely black* with a greenish gloss on upper surface. *Very long pinkish-red legs, very long fine black bill*, red eye. Juvenile has white on head, neck and breast, with black patch around eye and grey wash on back of neck. Wings, belly, flanks and undertail black. Full black plumage acquired over the first year, but throughout the bill is longer than in Pied Stilt and the legs slightly shorter. Naturally hybridises with Pied Stilt; adult hybrids are very variable, but longer bill and shorter legs are apparent in darker birds. Unlike juvenile Black Stilt, hybrid adults have some solid black on the breast. **Habitat:** Breeds on riverbeds, lake margins and ponds of Mackenzie Basin, inland South Canterbury. After breeding, most move to river deltas of major lakes in the Mackenzie Basin, but some move to estuaries of eastern South I and western North I. **Breeding:** Sep–Jan.

AUSTRALIAN RED-NECKED AVOCET *Recurvirostra novaehollandiae*

Rare Australian vagrant

44 cm, 300 g. Distinctive *black and white wader with chestnut head and neck, and fine upcurved bill* (more steeply in male) and long pale blue-grey legs. White body; black and white pattern on wings and back especially noticeable in flight. Juvenile has paler chestnut head and neck, and brown and white wing markings. *Feeds with scythe-like sweep of the bill*. **Habitat:** Formerly bred on South I riverbeds; now a vagrant to lakes and estuaries.

PIED STILT

imm

juv

BLACK STILT

imm

juv

id Black/Pied Stilts

AUSTRALIAN RED-NECKED
AVOCET

Plate 40 WADERS

BANDED DOTTEREL (Tuturiwhatu) *Charadrius bicinctus* Abundant endemic

20 cm, 60 g. Medium-sized dotterel with a confusing range of plumages according to age, sex and time of year. Breeding adult has white underparts except for *2 bands, a thin black band on the lower neck and a broad chestnut band on the breast*. Male has bolder and darker bands, and also has a thin black band above white forehead, and a dark line through eye. Non-breeding adults of both sexes are highly variable: black facial markings are lost; breast bands fade and often lost except as yellow to grey-brown tabs at the shoulders; upper band usually shows as a faint incomplete necklace of spots, but some retain a distinct upper band. Juvenile like non-breeding, but *whole head washed yellowish buff*, brown mottling on breast usually forms dark shoulder tabs, and upperparts grey-brown with fawn or off-white edges to the feathers. All have short dark grey bill, black legs or, variable yellowish-grey-green legs. Main calls a loud 'pit' and a fast rolling 'che-ree-a-ree'. **Habitat:** Breeds on sandy beaches, shellbanks and riverbeds. After breeding, form flocks at estuaries, lake margins and sometimes short grassland, e.g. airfields. Some, especially those breeding in high-country South I, migrate to Australia. **Breeding:** Jul–Jan.

NEW ZEALAND DOTTEREL (Tuturiwhatu) *Charadrius obscurus*
Uncommon endemic

25 cm, 160 g. *Large squat tame dotterel with large head and robust bill.* Breeding adult has upperparts brown, finely streaked dark brown, and whitish feather edges; *underparts range from pale orange-buff to rich rufous*; darker red in males and in southern subspecies (*obscurus*). Non-breeding adult is nondescript but *distinctly pale*; grey-brown upperparts have broad whitish feather edges; underparts white with obscure pale grey-brown breast band, often restricted to just the shoulders. Juvenile like a pale breeding adult but with buff feather edges and pale orange-buff wash on breast and belly, flecked dark brown on breast and flanks. In flight, white wingbar and white edges to rump and tail. Heavy black bill, tip slightly upturned; proportionately short olive-grey legs. Usual call a penetrating 'chip'. **Habitat:** Beaches, rivermouths and estuaries of northern NZ (*aquilonius*); also breeds on mountain tops of Stewart I (*obscurus*), after breeding moves to estuaries of Stewart I, Southland and Farewell Spit. **Breeding:** Aug–Feb.

MONGOLIAN DOTTEREL *Charadrius mongolus* Rare Asian migrant

20 cm, 60 g. *Medium-sized leggy dotterel with heavy short black bill.* Breeding adult has broad brick-red breast band with *thin black line on upper margin*, red extends onto nape and upper forehead; black facial mask sometimes with thin line down centre of forehead. Non-breeding like non-breeding Banded Dotterel and Large Sand Dotterel, separated only with care. *Forehead and eyebrow clean white*; upperparts *plain grey-brown*, greyer than Banded Dotterel; *conspicuous dark eye patch*; underparts white, with *broad grey shoulder tabs*, sometimes meeting to form a band on lower neck. In flight, distinct wingbar just onto primaries. Sexes alike. Usual call 'chirrip' with rolled 'r'. **Habitat:** Breeds Asia. Only a few reach NZ estuaries each year, most regularly at Manukau, Firth of Thames and Farewell Spit.

LARGE SAND DOTTEREL *Charadrius leschenaultii* Rare Asian migrant

24 cm, 90 g. *Large leggy dotterel with long heavy black bill.* Like Mongolian Dotterel but larger, much longer legs and body held more horizontal, and bill much more robust. Breeding adult has a narrow pale reddish-orange breast band, extending upwards on sides of neck to behind eye; black line through eye to bill and across top of forehead. Non-breeding has white forehead and eyebrow, *plain grey-brown upperparts* and white underparts except for grey-brown shoulder tabs, which may meet to form a thin breast band. Legs *long*, yellowish grey to green. In flight, distinct wingbar well onto primaries. Sexes alike. Usual call is a soft *trill*. **Habitat:** Breeds Central Asia. Only a few reach NZ estuaries each year, mostly at Kaipara, Manukau, Firth of Thames and Farewell Spit.

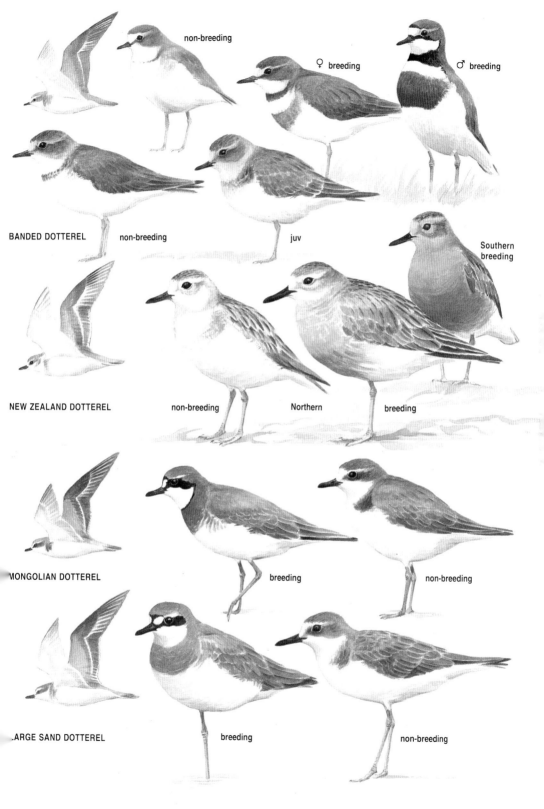

BANDED DOTTEREL

non-breeding

♀ breeding

♂ breeding

non-breeding

juv

NEW ZEALAND DOTTEREL

Southern breeding

non-breeding

Northern

breeding

MONGOLIAN DOTTEREL

breeding

non-breeding

LARGE SAND DOTTEREL

breeding

non-breeding

Plate 41   # WADERS

BLACK-FRONTED DOTTEREL   *Charadrius melanops*   Locally common native

17 cm, 33 g. Distinctive small dotterel with *slow jerky flight, black wingtips and metallic 'pit' flight call*. Upperparts mottled light brown with chestnut shoulder patch; black forehead, vertical patch onto crown, eyeline and *V-shaped breast band*; white eyebrow, side of neck and underparts. *Bill bright red, tipped black*; legs dull pink. Sexes alike. Juvenile lacks breast band, black forehead and shoulder patch. **Habitat:** Recently colonised from Australia. Breeds on riverbeds (especially near backwaters), gravel pits and bare ground. Form flocks after breeding, especially on lake margins and damp paddocks. **Breeding:** Aug–Mar.

SHORE PLOVER (Tuturuatu)   *Thinornis novaeseelandiae*   Rare endemic

20 cm, 60 g. Distinctive *small stocky dotterel* of South East I and the Western Reef in the Chathams, but recently introduced on Motuora I in the Hauraki Gulf and Portland I in Hawke's Bay, and seen on nearby estuaries. Crown, neck and upperparts greyish brown; white ring around back of head above eyes and across forecrown; black forehead, sides of face and throat in males, dirty brown in females; underparts white. Bill red, tipped black; legs orange. Juvenile has white head and neck with brown-grey cap and eye patch; bill brown with orange base. Usual call a quiet 'kleet', but loud ringing aggressive calls sound like oystercatcher piping calls. **Habitat:** Wave platforms, marsh-turf and estuaries. **Breeding:** Oct–Feb.

RED-KNEED DOTTEREL   *Erythrogonys cinctus*   Rare Australian vagrant

18 cm, 50 g. Distinctive dotterel with *broad white trailing edge to chocolate brown wings* and *white tail with dark central stripe*. Black head and breast band boldly contrasts with white chin and sides of neck. Back brown, underparts white with chestnut patch under bend of wing. Bill red, tipped black; long legs, pink above 'knee', grey below. Sexes alike. Juvenile has head grey-brown, breast band absent or smudgy grey-brown. **Habitat:** In Australia, usually feeds in freshwater or brackish wetlands. One NZ record: Manawatu Estuary, March 1976.

RED-CAPPED DOTTEREL   *Charadrius ruficapillus*   Rare Australian vagrant

15 cm, 38 g. Small active pale *greyish-brown dotterel with bright white underparts and black legs*, rufous head and nape, black bill and thin white wingbar. Male has white forehead edged black above, black line through eye edging rufous neck. Bill and legs black. Female has much less extensive rufous and lacks black markings. Juvenile duller and mottled above. **Habitat:** Formerly bred on shingle riverbeds of South I; now a rare vagrant.

RINGED PLOVER   *Charadrius hiaticula*   Rare Arctic vagrant

19 cm, 60 g. Small plump dotterel with a short stubby bill and a *white ring around neck* separating the brown nape from the back. Breeding adult has black breast band, eye patch, forecrown and line from eye to bill; bill orange, tipped black. Non-breeding has white forehead and pale buff eyebrow to well behind eye. Crown, eye patch, line to bill, back and breast band grey-brown. Bill black with dull orange base; orange legs. **Habitat:** Breeds Arctic. Two NZ records, at Firth of Thames.

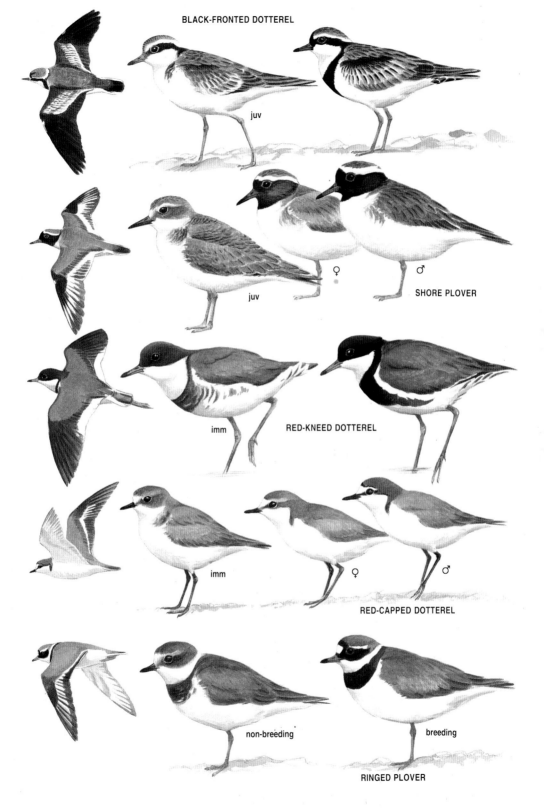

BLACK-FRONTED DOTTEREL

juv

juv

♀

♂

SHORE PLOVER

imm

RED-KNEED DOTTEREL

imm

♀

♂

RED-CAPPED DOTTEREL

non-breeding

breeding

RINGED PLOVER

Plate 42   **WADERS**

PACIFIC GOLDEN PLOVER   *Pluvialis fulva*   **Common Arctic migrant**

25 cm, 130 g. Medium-sized speckled wader, often in marsh-turf or short grass. Wary; when alert stands tall, looking slim with long neck and large head. Breeding adult has brown upperparts heavily speckled golden yellow and white; black face and underparts (*mottled on flanks*) separated by broad white stripe from bill, above eye and down neck to flanks. Non-breeding has head and upperparts pale brown with golden-buff or cream spots; tail barred brown and buff; pale buff eye stripe; throat and chest buff, speckled brown and yellow, grading into pale buff flanks, belly and undertail. Sexes alike. Juvenile has more heavily speckled upperparts and yellower head and underparts; more dark markings on breast and flanks. In flight, dark brown upperwing with an indistinct pale wingbar, and uniform brownish-grey underwing and armpits. At rest, tip of tertials level with tip of tail, and wings just longer than tail. Large black eye, short black bill. Long dark grey legs give leggy appearance. Flight fast and direct, often in small flocks. *Flight call a musical 'too-weet'*. **Habitat:** Breeds Arctic tundra of Siberia and W Alaska. In NZ, at estuaries with extensive *Zostera* and *Sarcocornia/Samolus* beds (especially Parengarenga, Manawatu, Farewell Spit, Awarua Bay) or freshwater wetlands with marsh-turf on fringes (Kaimaumau, Lakes Wairarapa and Ellesmere); rarely on short grassland in NZ. Very few overwinter.

AMERICAN GOLDEN PLOVER   *Pluvialis dominica*   **Rare Arctic vagrant**

26 cm, 165 g. Like Pacific Golden Plover but slightly *larger*, deeper chested with stouter bill and shorter legs (especially tibia). *Tip of tertials falls well short of tip of tail*, and wing usually much longer than tail. Breeding plumage male has *completely black flanks*; non-breeding adults and juveniles are *greyer* than Pacific Golden Plover, golden tones restricted to the back and scapulars. Juvenile has more mottling and barring on underparts, and ear coverts and cap are darker, making white eyebrow more prominent. **Habitat:** Breeds Arctic America. Migrates to inland S America. One confirmed NZ record.

GREY PLOVER   *Pluvialis squatarola*   **Uncommon Arctic migrant**

28 cm, 250 g. Much *larger heavier-billed and greyer than Pacific Golden Plover*. Has spangled appearance, and black face, throat and underparts in breeding plumage. Non-breeding is very pale, speckled grey and white head, upperparts and breast; white underparts. In flight, white underwings have diagnostic *black armpits*, thin white wingbar, *white rump*, and barred tail. Sexes alike. Juvenile grey-brown above with white and a few yellow spots. Large black eye, stout black bill and long ash-grey legs. Flight call a 3-note 'hee-oo-ee'. **Habitat:** Breeds high Arctic. In NZ, at estuaries, especially Parengarenga, Firth of Thames and Farewell Spit.

UPLAND SANDPIPER   *Bartramia longicauda*   **Rare American vagrant**

28 cm, 140 g. A brown-streaked wader with *large body, long slender neck, long tail, small head*, large black eye and short thin straight bill. Head, throat and upperparts olive-buff, streaked dark brown; flanks white with dark brown chevrons, abdomen white. In flight, rump and tail have dark centre and thin white or creamy margins, dark upperwing with black primaries. *Wings held upright on landing* to show pied barring on underwings. **Habitat:** Breeds N America. Migrates to S America. One NZ record.

ORIENTAL DOTTEREL   *Charadrius veredus*   **Rare Asian migrant**

24 cm, 95 g. Medium-sized plover with a *slim elegant build, long legs and an erect stance*. Breeding adult has broad chestnut breast band with black lower margin. Non-breeding has plain grey-brown upperparts, but some have narrow buff margins to feathers; pale buff eyebrow, face and throat, broad grey-buff breast band contrasts with off-white abdomen. Juvenile like non-breeding but broad pale margins to feathers on upperparts. In flight, no clear wingbar, underwing grey. Fine black bill; proportionately long dull yellow legs. **Habitat:** Breeds N China. In NZ, at estuaries, in areas of dried mud or short pasture, often with Banded Dotterel or Pacific Golden Plover.

PACIFIC GOLDEN PLOVER

breeding

juv

non-breeding

Pacific

moulting

AMERICAN
GOLDEN PLOVER

juv

GREY PLOVER

breeding

non-breeding

UPLAND SANDPIPER

breeding

ORIENTAL
DOTTEREL

non-breeding

Plate 43 WADERS

PAINTED SNIPE *Rostratula benghalensis* **Rare Australian vagrant**

25 cm, 120 g. Distinctive large-bodied chestnut, olive and white wader with short greenish legs and long (5 cm) slightly decurved bill. Buff stripe over centre of head from bill to nape; white band sweeps up in front of wings from breast to back; broad olive or buff and black patterned wings. Adult male has brown head with pale buff eye patch; nape, throat and breast streaked greyish brown; wings, back and uppertail spangled buff and grey; belly white. Adult female has maroon-brown head with white eye patch; reddish-brown nape, throat and breast; dark olive-grey wings, back and uppertail; white belly. When flushed, flies with slow wingbeats, legs dangle like in Pukeko, and gives repeated 'kuk' call. **Habitat:** Breeds Africa and Australasia. One NZ record, at Lake Ellesmere, August 1986. Usually in long grass near freshwater wetlands.

JAPANESE SNIPE *Gallinago hardwickii* **Rare Arctic migrant**

24 cm, 160 g. Richly variegated rotund brown wader with *very long (7 cm) straight bill*, short grey legs, heavily streaked head with large eyes set high on the head. *Fast zig-zagging flight when flushed* from thick cover near wetland margins; gives harsh call: 'kok'. Head streaked dark brown and buff; upperparts heavily streaked brown, buff and black; breast buff, speckled dark brown; flanks barred; belly and undertail creamy white. **Habitat:** Breeds Japan and eastern Russia. Migrates to Australasia. Only a few reach NZ, mainly in long grass near freshwater wetlands.

CHATHAM ISLAND SNIPE *Coenocorypha pusilla* **Locally common endemic**

20 cm, 80 g. Like NZ Snipe but smaller, shorter (3 cm) bill, and pale unmarked lower breast and belly. **Habitat:** Forest and thick vegetation on offshore islands in Chathams group, mainly South East and Mangere Is. **Breeding:** Sep–Feb.

NEW ZEALAND SNIPE (Hakawai) *Coenocorypha aucklandica*
Locally common endemic

23 cm, 105 g. Small rotund richly variegated brown wader with *long (5 cm) slightly drooping brown bill* and short yellowish-brown legs. Head marked boldly with buff central stripe over head from forehead to nape, long buff eyebrows and brown line through eye; pale buff cheek patch, streaked darker. Upperparts heavily mottled with black feather centres and brown or buff edges. Throat, neck and breast buff, streaked brown. Female larger than male. Male calls a low 'trerk trerk trerk' and 'queeyoo, queeyoo', but sometimes a *ghostly whistle at night* caused by vibrating tail feathers as air passes through the spread tail during aerial display. Confined to NZ subantarctic islands. **Habitat:** Forest and scrub of The Snares (*heugeli*), Antipodes (*meinertzhagenae*), and Ewing and Adams Is in the Auckland Is (*aucklandica*). **Breeding:** Aug–Feb.

PAINTED SNIPE

♀

♂

♀

JAPANESE SNIPE

Japanese
Snipe

NEW ZEALAND SNIPE

CHATHAM ISLAND SNIPE

Plate 44

WADERS

LESSER KNOT (Huahou)   *Calidris canutus*   Abundant Arctic migrant

24 cm, 120 g. A stocky rather nondescript wader with a heavy (3 cm) straight black bill and short dull green legs, but distinctive rusty red head and underparts in breeding plumage. Head and upperparts of non-breeding adult plain grey with paler feather edges, whitish eyebrow; underparts pale grey to off-white, with lightly speckled grey on neck, breast and flanks. Head, neck and breast of breeding adult become *rusty red*, and back black with rust and white speckling; females less richly coloured. Juvenile like non-breeding, but back more scaly with white feather tips and subterminal black lines. In flight, indistinct white wingbar, *pale rump barred white and grey*. Often seen in flocks and with Bar-tailed Godwits. **Habitat:** Breeds Arctic. Second most common migrant visiting NZ estuaries each summer; many over-winter. Favours northern and western estuaries, especially Kaipara, Manukau, Firth of Thames and Farewell Spit; only occasionally on margins of freshwater lakes.

GREAT KNOT   *Calidris tenuirostris*   Rare Arctic migrant

27 cm, 160 g. Like Lesser Knot but larger, with a *heavier longer (4 cm) black bill and white rump*. Head and upperparts of non-breeding adult plain grey with paler feather edges, finely streaked dark grey on crown, neck and breast; indistinct eyebrow; flanks usually marked with *dark arrowhead-shaped spots*. Breeding adult has head and neck heavily streaked black; breast very heavily blotched blackish brown, extending onto flanks as bold arrowhead-shaped spots; rusty-red feathers on base of upperwing only. Juvenile like non-breeding, but back and wing feathers have darker centres with buff fringes; brownish-buff wash on breast. **Habitat:** Breeds Siberia. Migrates to Australasia. Only a few reach NZ, normally with Lesser Knots at northern or western estuaries.

CURLEW SANDPIPER   *Calidris ferruginea*   Uncommon Arctic migrant

19 cm, 60 g. A small slender wader with *long thin downcurved bill*, black legs, *white rump* and white wingbar. Non-breeding adult has *pale* plain grey-brown head and upperparts; white eyebrow; underparts white with pale grey wash and streaks on breast. Breeding adult has distinctive rusty-red head and underparts, with feathers initially edged white; back feathers black, notched grey and rust red. Juvenile like non-breeding, but back feathers darker, edged white, and lightly streaked neck and breast washed buff. **Habitat:** Breeds Arctic Asia. Regular summer visitor to NZ, and some overwinter. Favours tidal flats, brackish pools and margins to coastal lakes, mainly at Firth of Thames, Lake Ellesmere and Awarua Bay.

DUNLIN   *Calidris alpina*   Rare Arctic straggler

18 cm, 50 g. Like Curlew Sandpiper but shorter legs, *a shorter only slightly downcurved bill, and black central stripe through white rump*. Non-breeding adult browner with buff-washed upper breast, and less distinct eyebrow. Breeding adult has rusty red on crown and edges of dark-centred back feathers, breast and flanks streaked black, *belly black*, and undertail white. **Habitat:** Breeds Holarctic. Migrates to northern tropics. A few have reached northern NZ estuaries in summer.

WHITE-RUMPED SANDPIPER   *Calidris fuscicollis*   Rare Arctic vagrant

16 cm, 35 g. Small slender wader with short black legs, short slightly drooping black bill, usually with pale base to lower mandible; *white rump*. Folded wings project well beyond tail to give elongated appearance. Non-breeding adult has drab grey head and upperparts with paler feather edges, neck and breast streaked and washed grey; underparts off-white. Breeding adult has dark streaked head, washed pale rufous on crown and ear coverts; rufous fringes to feathers of back and inner wing; breast heavily streaked brown, often extending onto flanks as chevrons. In flight, narrow white wingbar. **Habitat:** Breeds Arctic N America. Migrates to S America. A few have reached NZ estuaries.

juv

non-breeding

breeding

LESSER KNOT

non-breeding

breeding

GREAT KNOT

breeding

CURLEW SANDPIPER

non-breeding

breeding

DUNLIN

non-breeding

breeding

WHITE-RUMPED SANDPIPER

non-breeding

Plate 45

WADERS

WRYBILL *Anarhynchus frontalis*

Locally common endemic

20 cm, 60 g. Very pale grey stocky confiding wader with short thick neck and black bill with *tip curved to the right*. Legs grey-green. Breeding adult has white forehead edged above with thin black frontal band in male; crown, nape and upperparts plain ashy grey. Underparts white except *black band across upper breast*, narrower in female. Non-breeding lacks frontal band, and breast band is indistinct or absent. Juvenile has back feathers edged white, and breast band always absent. In flight, small white wingbar and white sides to grey rump. Form dense flocks at roosts, usually apart from most other waders. **Habitat:** Breeds shingle riverbeds of Canterbury and Otago. Migrates to estuaries of North I, especially Firth of Thames, Manukau and Kaipara. Feeds on wet mudflats. **Breeding:** Aug–Jan.

TURNSTONE *Arenaria interpres*

Common Arctic migrant

23 cm, 120 g. Very striking stout wader with *variegated white, black, brown and tortoise-shell plumage*, short black bill and *short orange legs*. Horizontal stance and habit of busily fossicking along the tideline, probing under debris and bulldozing or flicking over tide-wrack. Non-breeding has head and upperparts dark brown, mottled black and chestnut; face variegated black, white and brown; upperbreast black, underparts white. In breeding plumage, male more boldly marked with white cap, finely streaked black; female has brown cap, streaked black and white. In flight, striking complex pattern of black, white and chestnut. **Habitat:** Breeds high Arctic. In NZ, favours wave platforms, coastal lagoons and some estuaries, especially Parengarenga, Kaipara, Farewell Spit, Motueka, Lake Grassmere, Kaikoura Peninsula, Awarua Bay and Te Whanga Lagoon (Chathams).

TEREK SANDPIPER *Tringa terek*

Uncommon Arctic migrant

23 cm, 70 g. Plain pale grey-brown wader with *long thin upcurved black bill with orange base, short orange-yellow legs*, and dark patch at bend of wing. Moves actively with crouched run and bobs head and tail. Non-breeding has head and upperparts pale brownish grey with faint white eyebrow; throat and breast variably streaked grey; underparts white. Breeding has browner back, finely flecked grey, and black streak at base of upperwing appears as a black line along back. In flight, *broad white trailing edge to upperwing* near body, pale sides to rump and tail. **Habitat:** Breeds Eurasia. A few reach NZ estuaries each summer, often roosting with Wrybills.

SANDERLING *Calidris alba*

Rare Arctic migrant

20 cm, 50 g. Very pale wader with *black patch at bend of wing*, short stout black bill and short black legs. *Feeds actively; runs along water edge on sandy beaches*. Non-breeding has head and back pearly grey; sides of face white with grey wash through eye; underparts white. Breeding has head, breast and upper back pale rusty red, speckled black. Juvenile like non-breeding but back scalloped black and grey, and head and sides of lower neck streaked black. In flight, *prominent white wingbar*, enhanced by dark grey leading edge and tips to wing; black stripe down centre of tail; white sides to rump and grey sides to tail. **Habitat**: Breeds Arctic. A few reach NZ each summer, on sandy beaches and estuaries.

COMMON SANDPIPER *Tringa hypoleucos*

Rare Arctic migrant

20 cm, 50 g. Small dark solitary sandpiper with *white tab in front of folded wing. Often perches on rocks or logs and bobs head and tips tail. Jerky, flickering flight interspersed with glides on stiffly held wings*. Head and upperparts olive brown except white eye-ring and eyebrow, boldest in front of eye; throat and sides of neck washed brown; underparts white. Tail long, extending well beyond folded wings. Short straight dark brown bill; short greenish-grey legs. In flight, white wingbar and white sides to brown rump and tail. Flight call a distinctive clear 'hee-dee-dee'. **Habitat:** Breeds Eurasia. A few reach NZ, usually in small muddy estuaries.

WRYBILL

non-breeding

♀ breeding

♂ breeding

TURNSTONE

♂ breeding

non-breeding

♀ breeding

TEREK SANDPIPER

breeding

non-breeding

SANDERLING

breeding

juv

non-breeding

Sanderling

COMMON SANDPIPER

Plate 46

WADERS

SHARP-TAILED SANDPIPER *Calidris acuminata* Uncommon Arctic migrant

22 cm, 60 g. A medium-small richly speckled brown wader with *rufous crown*, finely streaked black, and white eyebrow. Bill (2.5 cm) slightly downcurved, *grey-brown with greenish base. Legs yellowish green*. Non-breeding has upperparts dull brown with pale feather edges; neck and breast mottled grey or buffish with irregular streaks, *fading* to white on lower breast and belly. In breeding plumage, upperparts richly coloured with chestnut and buff edges to feathers; breast heavily streaked and marked with *small boomerang-shaped streaks on lower breast and along flanks*. Juvenile like non-breeding adult but more rufous, especially on crown, neck and *edges of tertials*. In flight, faint white wingbar and white sides to black rump and uppertail. **Habitat:** Breeds Siberia. Migrates to Australasia. In NZ, favours low-growing saltmarsh of estuaries and open marsh-turf flats of coastal lakes, mainly at Kaimaumau, Firth of Thames, Ahuriri and Manawatu Estuaries, Lakes Wairarapa and Ellesmere, and Awarua Bay.

PECTORAL SANDPIPER *Calidris melanotos* Rare Arctic migrant

23 cm, 80 g. Non-breeding like Sharp-tailed Sandpiper, but darker, *crown streaked brown and buff*, neck and breast *heavily streaked dark brown that ends abruptly* and contrasts with white underparts. Bill (2.5 cm) slightly downcurved, *brown with yellowish base; legs yellow*. In breeding plumage, upperparts become darker, with chestnut and buff feather edges; breast heavily streaked in male, blackish brown flecked white in female. Juvenile like non-breeding adult but more rufous on head and back. In flight, faint white wingbar and white sides to black rump and uppertail. **Habitat:** Breeds Arctic N America. Migrates to S America. A few reach NZ each summer, often with Sharp-tailed Sandpipers on open marsh-turf flats of coastal lakes, especially Lakes Wairarapa and Ellesmere, or in low-growing saltmarsh of estuaries.

RUFF (Reeve) *Philomachus pugnax* Rare Arctic vagrant

29 cm, 170 g. Non-breeding like large *upright* Sharp-tailed Sandpiper, but lacks rufous crown and has *small head, short fine bill, long neck and legs*. Head and upperparts scaly grey-brown with grey feather edges, wings darker; throat and sides of face white; breast buff, washed grey brown; belly, undertail and underwings white. Bill (3.5 cm) slightly downcurved, brown with paler base. Legs from orange to green. Breeding plumage (not recorded in NZ) is highly variable, especially in males, which have many colours and large neck ruffs and head tufts; female like non-breeding but dark barring on upperparts and black blotches on breast. Juvenile like non-breeding but upperparts have buff feather edges and neck and breast washed buff. In flight, looks long-winged with narrow white wingbar; *prominent white oval patches on sides of rump*. **Habitat:** Breeds Arctic. Straggles to Australasia. Only a few NZ records, mainly at margins of freshwater or brackish lakes.

BAIRD'S SANDPIPER *Calidris bairdii* Rare Arctic vagrant

18 cm, 40 g. Small buff-brown wader with *straight fine black bill*, short black legs, *broad black centre to white rump and tail*, and *long wings that project well beyond tail*, giving it an elongated look. Complete finely streaked buff breast band. Non-breeding adult has head and upperparts uniformly scaly brown, with buff feather edges. In breeding plumage, crown and breast become strongly streaked dark brown, upperparts dark brown and black with white feather edges, and some rufous on the back. Juvenile has rusty brown upperparts and chest; pale edges to feathers give a scaly effect on the back and wings. In flight, a very narrow short wingbar. **Habitat:** Breeds Arctic N America. Migrates to S America. A few reach NZ estuaries.

SHARP-TAILED SANDPIPER

breeding

non-breeding

juv

PECTORAL SANDPIPER

non-breeding

juv

RUFF

♀ moulting

juv

♂ non-breeding

BAIRD'S SANDPIPER

juv

ad non-breeding

Plate 47

WADERS

RED-NECKED STINT   *Calidris ruficollis*   **Common Arctic migrant**

15 cm, 30 g. Tiny wader with short straight black bill and short black legs. Non-breeding adult has forehead and eyebrow white; crown, neck and upperparts *pale grey* with brownish tinge, paler feather edges and black feather shafts. Breeding adult has crown and back blackish brown with rufous feather edges, *contrasting* with grey-brown pale-edged feathers on wing coverts; *sides of face, neck, chin and throat brick red*; underparts white. Juvenile like non-breeding, but crown and sides of breast washed pale rufous; back feathers dark rufous-edged, contrasting with greyer pale-edged wing coverts. Some show thin white V on back and double white eyebrow. In flight, white wingbar reaches base of primaries; white sides to uppertail contrast with black central stripe down rump and tail. Feeds by pecking with rapid sewing-machine action. **Habitat:** Breeds Siberia and Alaska. Migrates to Australasia. Several hundred reach NZ in summer, and some overwinter. Mainly at estuaries and coastal lakes, especially at Parengarenga, Manukau, Porangahau, Farewell Spit, Lake Ellesmere and Awarua Bay.

LITTLE STINT   *Calidris minuta*   **Rare Arctic vagrant**

15 cm, 25 g. Tiny wader, like Red-necked Stint but slightly smaller, slightly longer black legs, and slightly longer bill, decurved at the tip; shorter wings give less attenuated rear end. Non-breeding adult has upperpart feathers dark-centred, edged brown, giving a browner appearance. Breeding adult has head, neck and upper breast *orange-rufous*, streaked and mottled darker; *chin and throat white*; back dark brown with creamy-white V-shaped line, broad orange-rufous feather edges and *no contrast between back and wing coverts*. Juvenile has upperpart feathers with *broad orange-rufous fringes, a prominent white V on the back* and a double eyebrow. In flight, white wingbar does not reach primaries; white sides to black stripe down rump and tail. **Habitat:** Breeds Arctic Eurasia. Migrates to Europe, Africa and Asia. Rare vagrants have reached Lake Ellesmere.

LEAST SANDPIPER   *Calidris minutilla*   **Rare Arctic vagrant**

15 cm, 25 g. Tiny wader, like Red-necked Stint but browner and with *dull yellow legs*, and more crouched bent-legged feeding posture. Very difficult to identify from slightly larger Long-toed Stint (*C. subminuta*) seen regularly in Australia. Shrill *'kreep-keep-keep'* call and thicker all black bill are best field features of Least Stint; also crown paler and more streaked, dark line from bill to eye, and heavily streaked breast. In flight, narrow white wingbar, and white sides to thin black line down rump. **Habitat:** Breeds Arctic N America. Migrates to S America. One record in NZ (Wairoa 1952), but several other yellow-legged stints have been recorded.

BROAD-BILLED SANDPIPER   *Limicola falcinellus*   **Rare Arctic migrant**

17 cm, 35 g. Small wader with short *olive-green legs, very long (3 cm) heavy black bill* slightly drooped at tip, and *double eyebrow; a broad white eyebrow joining a thinner, higher stripe in front of each eye*. Non-breeding adult has crown, neck and upperparts pale brown-grey with dark feather shafts and pale edges giving a scaly appearance; grey stripe down centre of head to bill; underparts white, lightly streaked grey on sides of neck and breast. Breeding adult has head, neck and breast streaked black; upperparts very dark, feathers thinly edged buff or rufous, giving a streaked appearance; central stripe on head becomes black. Juvenile has prominent V on mantle, rufous edges to mantle and inner scapulars, buff and white edges to rest of upperparts. In flight, dark grey leading edges to upperwing and narrow white wingbar; white sides to rump contrast with broad dark grey stripe down centre of tail. **Habitat:** Breeds Arctic Eurasia. Migrates to SE Asia. Scarce visitor to NZ estuaries.

WESTERN SANDPIPER   *Calidris mauri*   **Rare Arctic vagrant**

17 cm, 30 g. Tiny wader with short black legs, like Red-necked Stint but with distinctly *longer (2.5 cm) slightly drooping black bill*. Non-breeding adult has pale grey upperparts with paler feather edges, white eyebrow, breast finely streaked grey, underparts white. Breeding adult has rufous crown, nape and patch behind eye, prominent white eyebrow; back grey-brown, mottled rufous and black on scapulars; breast and flanks marked with black streaks and chevrons. Juvenile like breeding adult but paler rufous on head; breast washed buff and lightly streaked black at sides. In flight, narrow white wingbar, white sides to black rump. **Habitat:** Breeds Arctic N America and eastern Siberia. Migrates to Central America. A few reach NZ estuaries.

RED-NECKED STINT   breeding   non-breeding

juv

LITTLE STINT   breeding   non-breeding

juv

Little
Stint

EAST SANDPIPER   non-breeding

BROAD-BILLED
SANDPIPER   breeding   non-breeding

WESTERN
SANDPIPER   breeding   non-breeding

Plate 48
WADERS

EASTERN CURLEW *Numenius madagascariensis* **Uncommon Arctic migrant**

63 cm, 900 g. Largest wader in NZ. Distinctive *very long (19 cm) downcurved bill*. Body streaked greyish brown and buff, paler on underparts, with indistinct white eyebrow and brown rump. Bill dark brown with pink base to lower bill. *Flight call a distinctive carrying 'croo-lee'*. **Habitat:** Breeds northeastern Asia. Migrates to Australasia; c. 30 visit NZ each summer, mainly at Firth of Thames and Farewell Spit.

WHIMBREL *Numenius phaeopus* **Uncommon Arctic migrant**

43 cm, 450 g. Medium-sized curlew with *long (9 cm) downcurved bill,* head marked boldly with white eyebrows and centre stripe over top of dark brown head. Asiatic subspecies (*variegata*) has *off-white rump.* American subspecies (*hudsonicus*) has *speckled brown rump.* Body completely streaked greyish brown and buff. Bill black, legs bluish grey. *Flight call a rippling whistle of about 7 notes: 'ti-ti-ti-ti-ti-ti-ti'.* Often very wary and stands alert near roosting flocks of waders. **Habitat:** Breeds Arctic. 100–200 visit NZ each summer (mainly Asiatic), especially at Parengarenga, Firth of Thames and Farewell Spit.

BRISTLE-THIGHED CURLEW *Numenius tahitiensis* **Rare Arctic straggler**

43 cm, 400 g. Medium-sized *buff and brown* curlew with *long (9 cm) downcurved bill and very boldly marked head.* Dark eye stripe, pale buff eyebrow and central stripe over top of dark brown head. Body streaked brown and buff; *rump smooth cinnamon;* tail rusty buff, barred black; belly whitish, and upper legs have a few long loose white feathers. *Flight call a clear 'kee-vee',* unlike trilling call of other curlews. **Habitat:** Breeds western Alaska. Common migrant to central Pacific. Only a few straggle to NZ, all records from the Kermadecs.

LITTLE WHIMBREL *Numenius minutus* **Rare Arctic migrant**

29 cm, 160 g. *Small curlew* with *long (5 cm) downcurved bill* and boldly marked head. Dark eye stripe, buff eyebrow and thin central stripe over top of brown head. Body streaked brown and warm buff, brown rump, and upperwing in flight looks dark and unmottled. Bill dark brown, pink base to lower bill; legs bluish grey. *Flight call a 3-note 'te-te-te'.* **Habitat:** Breeds Siberia. Migrates to Australasia. A rare visitor to NZ, mostly in short pasture or ploughed ground, often with Banded Dotterels or rather similar-looking Golden Plovers.

EASTERN CURLEW

American

Asiatic

WHIMBREL

BRISTLE-THIGHED
CURLEW

LITTLE WHIMBREL

Plate 49

WADERS

BAR-TAILED GODWIT (Kuaka) *Limosa lapponica* Abundant Arctic migrant

♂ 39 cm, 300 g; ♀ 41 cm, 350 g. Commonest migrant wader. Long (♂ 8.5 cm, ♀ 10.5 cm) *slightly upturned black bill with a pink base*. Legs and feet black. Non-breeding has head, upperparts and upperwings streaked grey-brown; lower back, *rump and tail barred brown and white*; underparts dirty white, washed grey on breast; underwings extensively flecked dark brown. Breeding adult, seen from February onwards, has black and buff upperparts; brick-red head, neck, breast and underparts in males; buffy red with fine barring in females. Juvenile like non-breeding but buffer and with more heavily marked upperparts, but unmarked breast. In flight, wingbar indistinct, pale rump and barred tail. Flies fast with twisting and turning, or direct in long lines or chevrons. **Habitat:** Breeds Arctic in Eurasia and Alaska. Eastern race *baueri* migrates to Australasia, especially NZ estuaries, sandy beaches and shores of coastal lakes. Main sites, where 10,000+ spend the southern summer, are Kaipara, Manukau and Farewell Spit.

HUDSONIAN GODWIT *Limosa haemastica* Rare Arctic migrant

39 cm, 300 g. In non-breeding plumage like Bar-tailed Godwit, but *smooth* grey upperparts and grey wash on breast. Conspicuous *white rump contrasts with broad black tip to the tail; narrow white wingbar*. Black armpits and extensive black on underwing separate from non-breeding Black-tailed Godwit. Breeding adult male has head and neck finely barred black and white, upperparts dark brown spotted buff, breast and belly chestnut; female paler on breast and belly. **Habitat:** Breeds N America. Migrates to S America. Vagrants reach NZ most summers, usually with Bar-tailed Godwits at estuaries.

BLACK-TAILED GODWIT *Limosa limosa* Rare Arctic migrant

39 cm, 350 g. In non-breeding plumage like Bar-tailed Godwit, but more elegant with *smooth* grey plumage and *long straight bill*. In flight, conspicuous *white wingbars, and white rump contrasts with broad black tip to the tail*. *White underwings and armpits with thin black margins* separate from non-breeding Hudsonian Godwit. Breeding adult has head, neck and breast brick red; belly barred black and white; upperparts mottled rusty and black. **Habitat:** Breeds temperate Eurasia. Race *melanuroides* migrates to Asia and Australasia. Only a few reach NZ each summer, usually with Bar-tailed Godwits at estuaries or with Pied Stilts on lake margins.

ASIATIC DOWITCHER *Limnodromus semipalmatus* Rare Asian vagrant

34 cm, 180 g. Like a small godwit but with *short legs* and a *long (8 cm), straight stout black bill*. In non-breeding plumage, face clearly marked with white eyebrow and dark line from bill to eye. Upperparts dark grey-brown, streaked paler; back, rump and tail barred brown and off-white; underparts flecked grey on breast and along flanks, belly white and *underwings mainly white*. Feeds with sewing-machine action of rapid probes with bill pointed straight down. **Habitat:** Breeds Central Asia. Migrates to S Asia and Australasia. Rarely reaches NZ estuaries.

BAR-TAILED GODWIT

juv

♂ breeding

♀ non-breeding

HUDSONIAN GODWIT

♂ breeding

non-breeding

BLACK-TAILED GODWIT

juv

♂ breeding

non-breeding

ASIATIC DOWITCHER

non-breeding

Plate 50 # WADERS

MARSH SANDPIPER *Tringa stagnatilis* Uncommon Arctic migrant

22 cm, 70 g. Elegant *pale grey* wader, like small Greenshank but *very long greenish legs* and *needle-like (4 cm) black bill.* Non-breeding has crown and eye stripe streaked grey, eyebrow white, upperparts ash grey, *darker at shoulder.* Underparts white. Breeding adult has head and neck flecked dark grey, upperparts brownish grey heavily barred and spotted dark brown, breast spotted dark brown and black; legs can turn yellowish. In flight, *lacks wingbar, white rump extends as a V well up back*; tail white, lightly barred grey in centre. Wades in shallow water and feeds with *head-down, tail-up, triangular stance.* **Habitat:** Breeds Central Asia. Reaches NZ estuaries and lake margins each summer, often with Pied Stilts.

GREENSHANK *Tringa nebularia* Uncommon Arctic migrant

32 cm, 170 g. Large elegant grey wader with long (5.5 cm) heavy *slightly upturned bill, blue-grey at base*; long green legs. Non-breeding has head and neck finely streaked grey, indistinct white eyebrow, upperparts dark grey, lightly flecked white and black; underparts white. Breeding adult has head, neck and upperbreast heavily flecked blackish brown; irregular dark mottling on upperparts. In flight, *lacks wingbar, white rump extends as a V well up back*; tail white, broadly barred dark grey. Wades in shallow water with *horizontal stance.* Distinctive voice, a loud ringing *'tew-tew-tew'.* **Habitat:** Breeds Eurasia. A few reach NZ each summer, often associated with Pied Stilts in muddy estuarine creeks and on lake margins.

LESSER YELLOWLEGS *Tringa flavipes* Rare Arctic vagrant

24 cm, 75 g. Elegant grey wader, like Marsh Sandpiper but *long slender yellow legs*, and *lower back greyish brown.* Bill (4 cm) fine and straight, slightly longer than head. Non-breeding has upperparts brownish grey, *white eyebrow only in front of eye*; wing feathers pale-edged giving a spotted look; underparts white except upper breast streaked brownish grey. Juvenile like non-breeding, but upperparts browner, strongly spotted white; neck and breast spotted and streaked brown. In flight, lacks wingbar, *square white rump not extending up back.* **Habitat:** Breeds N America. Migrates to S America. Occasionally recorded at NZ estuaries and lake margins.

WANDERING TATTLER *Tringa incana* Uncommon Arctic migrant

27 cm, 120 g. Medium-sized wader with smooth slate-grey back and *short yellow legs.* Like Siberian Tattler but call a clear *rippling trill of 6–10 notes.* Bill grey, *nasal groove extends 70% of length.* Non-breeding has head, upperparts and upperbreast slate grey, *white eyebrow only in front of eye*, underparts white. Breeding adult has all underparts, including flanks and undertail, heavily barred dark grey. In flight, smooth grey upperparts; flies on stiffly held wings. When alert, bobs head and tips tail. **Habitat:** Breeds western N America. Migrates to Central America and Pacific Is. A few regularly reach NZ estuaries and especially rocky shores each summer.

SIBERIAN (Grey-tailed) TATTLER *Tringa brevipes* Uncommon Arctic migrant

25 cm, 100 g. Like Wandering Tattler, but call a sharp high-pitched *'too-weet'.* Usually slightly paler and browner, and *white eyebrow extends behind eye* and as a thin line over the base of the bill. Bill grey, *nasal groove extends 50% of length.* In breeding plumage, underparts heavily barred dark grey, but flanks and undertail remain white. In flight, smooth grey-brown upperparts; flies on stiffly held wings. When alert, bobs head and tips tail. **Habitat:** Breeds Siberia. Migrates to Australasia. A few reach NZ estuaries and sometimes rocky shores each summer.

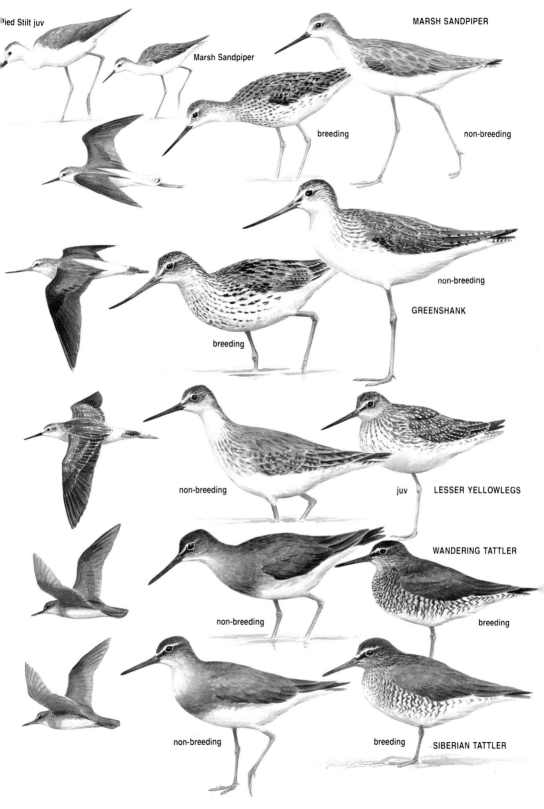

Pied Stilt juv

Marsh Sandpiper

MARSH SANDPIPER

breeding

non-breeding

non-breeding

GREENSHANK

breeding

non-breeding

juv

LESSER YELLOWLEGS

WANDERING TATTLER

non-breeding

breeding

non-breeding

breeding

SIBERIAN TATTLER

Plate 51 WADERS

RED-NECKED PHALAROPE   *Phalaropus lobatus*   Rare Arctic straggler

19 cm; ♂ 30 g, ♀ 35 g. Unusual small slim and graceful wader. *Feeds by swimming jerkily or in circles, pecking from the water surface. Short very fine black bill;* very short dark grey legs with lobed feet; white wingbar; large white patches at sides of rump contrast with black stripe down grey-tipped tail. Non-breeding adult like Grey Phalarope, but bill finer, back feathers have dark centres and broad white edges, giving a *scaly* appearance. Breeding adult unmistakable: mainly grey above, with rufous patch sweeping from behind eye down sides of neck to throat; male duller. Juvenile has grey patch behind and below eye, and grey on crown extends down hindneck to back. **Habitat:** Breeds Arctic. Migrates to pelagic waters off western N America, Arabia, Micronesia and Namibia. A few have straggled to NZ estuaries or coastal lakes.

GREY (Red) PHALAROPE   *Phalaropus fulicarius*   Rare Arctic vagrant

20 cm; ♂ 50 g, ♀ 60 g. Unusual dainty wader. *Feeds by swimming jerkily or in circles, pecking from the water surface. Short thick black bill* (yellow with black tip in breeding adult); short brownish-grey legs with yellow lobes on feet; white wingbar; small white patches at sides to grey tail. Non-breeding adult like non-breeding Red-necked Phalarope but bill stouter, back feathers have very thin white edges giving a *smooth* appearance. Breeding adult unmistakable: neck and underparts mainly brick red, back black and buff, and white patch around back of head behind eye; male duller. Juvenile initially a warm pinkish buff but quickly becomes like non-breeding adult; however, retains buff edges to wing feathers. **Habitat:** Breeds Arctic. Migrates to pelagic areas of tropical Atlantic Ocean, off Namibia and S America. A few have reached NZ estuaries and coastal lakes.

WILSON'S PHALAROPE   *Phalaropus tricolor*   Rare American vagrant

22 cm; ♂ 50 g, ♀ 65 g. Unusual slim and graceful wader. *Feeds by swimming jerkily or in circles pecking at the water surface,* or by wading, or running actively with *waddling gait on dry land with short yellow legs. Long needle-like black bill,* no wingbar, and *white rump* distinguish from other phalaropes. Non-breeding adult resembles small very short-legged Marsh Sandpiper, with very pale grey head and upperparts, darker on wings and back; white eyebrow and underparts. Breeding adult unmistakable: silver-grey and chestnut head, neck and upperparts on female; male duller and lacks grey areas. **Habitat:** Breeds N America. Migrates to wetlands of S America. Rare vagrant to NZ estuaries and lakes.

ORIENTAL PRATINCOLE   *Glareola maldivarum*   Rare Asian migrant

23 cm, 75 g. Distinctive atypical wader with *graceful buoyant tern-like flight while feeding by hawking,* swooping and soaring; sometimes feeds on ground with rapid tip-toeing run. Non-breeding adult has dull olive-brown crown, back and upperwings; throat buff, enclosed by a streaked black necklace; neck and upper breast pale olive-grey-brown, lower breast and belly white. Breeding adult has brighter olive-brown on head and upperparts; throat enclosed by bold black necklace; lower breast becomes buff. Juvenile has flecked appearance from back and upper breast feathers being tipped dark and edged buff. In flight, *underwing chestnut with dark grey trailing edge and tip, deeply forked white tail with olive brown tip.* **Habitat:** Breeds SE Asia. Migrates to Australasia, occasionally reaching NZ estuaries, coastal lakes and over open grassland.

RED-NECKED PHALAROPE

juv

♂ breeding

♀ breeding

non-breeding

GREY PHALAROPE

♂ breeding

♀ breeding

non-breeding

juv

WILSON'S PHALAROPE

♂ breeding

♀ breeding

non-breeding

imm

ORIENTAL PRATINCOLE   non-breeding   breeding

Plate 52

SKUAS

A small group of widespread and highly mobile coastal or marine birds, medium to large. Plumages are highly variable but mainly brown and white, with white flashes in the outer wing. The small skuas are difficult to separate during moult from juvenile to immature, or immature to adult plumages, or between breeding and non-breeding plumages. Sexes alike. Flight is fast and direct, or twisting and turning in pursuit while relentlessly chasing terns and gulls to force them to drop or disgorge food. Strongly territorial when breeding, and aggressively defend their territory from intruders. Usually lay 2 brown eggs in a shallow scrape or cup of vegetation.

ARCTIC SKUA   *Stercorarius parasiticus*   **Common Arctic migrant**

43 cm (+ projecting tail feathers), 400 g. Small elegant skua with highly variable plumages: two main phases (about 80% dark in NZ), intermediates and a wide range of juvenile and immature plumages. Difficult to distinguish from larger Pomarine Skua unless in mixed groups 'working' a flock of terns. Bill black; *legs and feet black* in adults, *or grey-blue tipped black* in juveniles. Dark phase breeding adult is blackish brown with slightly paler yellowish nape and ear coverts; pale phase has black cap, white cheeks, yellowish nape and ear coverts; brown back, wings and tail, white underparts with variable dark breast band and dark undertail. Continuous variation between; all adults have *dark underwing with single pale patch at base of primaries*, upperparts uniformly dark except for *3–4 pale shafts at base of primaries*, and *pointed central tail feathers project 10 cm beyond rest of tail*. Non-breeding similar but lacks tail projection; dark phase can have white flecks on rump; pale phase has less distinct cap, underparts and flanks barred and washed brown, *undertail streaked*, pale flecks on rump and uppertail. Juvenile highly variable, but all have barred underwings with *single pale patch* and upperwings as in adults; most have rusty-brown body, mottled and barred darker, and paler streaked neck. Immatures acquire adult plumage over several years; mostly like non-breeding adult, but pale phase more heavily barred and washed brown on underparts and face, and rump and undertail lightly barred; *rump is darker than the neck*. **Habitat:** Breeds Arctic and subarctic. Migrates to southern oceans. Commonest skua seen off NZ coast and in harbours, especially Jan–Apr, when often seen harrying slightly smaller White-fronted Terns or Red-billed Gulls. Sometimes roosts on beaches.

POMARINE SKUA   *Stercorarius pomarinus*   **Uncommon Arctic migrant**

48 cm (+ projecting tail feathers), 600 g. Similar range of plumages and pattern of plumage changes with age as Arctic Skua, but larger, *more heavily built and broader-winged; underwing dark with two pale patches at base of primaries*; upperwing shows 3-4 pale shafts on primaries. Breeding adult has twisted pair of tail feathers with *broad blunt ends* projecting 10 cm beyond rest of tail. Juvenile and immature have *rump paler than the neck*. Flight similar to Arctic Skua but less dashing as twisting and turning after distinctly smaller White-fronted Terns and Red-billed Gulls; direct flight with slower steadier wingbeats. **Habitat:** Breeds Arctic. Winters in tropics and southern oceans, especially off W Africa and eastern Australia. Regularly summer and autumn visitor to NZ coast, especially open coasts, e.g. Manawatu coast, Farewell Spit; rarely in harbours.

LONG-TAILED SKUA   *Stercorarius longicaudus*   **Rare Arctic migrant**

35 cm (+ projecting tail feathers), 300 g. Smallest skua. Like small slender Arctic Skua but more *buoyant tern-like flight; greyer upperparts with darker primaries, which have only 1–2 pale shafts; legs short and blue*. Similar variety of plumages and changes with age as in Arctic Skua. Pale phase usual in NZ, dark phase rare, and intermediates very rare. Breeding adult has greyish-brown upperparts contrasting with dark brown primaries and trailing edge to secondaries; very long and thin central *tail streamers project 20 cm beyond rest of tail*. Non-breeding adult lacks or has short pointed tail projection, and undertail is barred brown and white. Juvenile and immature have short tail projection, heavily barred underwing and undertail, and often a barred rump. **Habitat:** Breeds Arctic and subarctic. Winters in tropical and southern temperate oceans. Mostly straggles to North I, sometimes in moderate numbers.

ad light phase
non-breeding

ARCTIC SKUA

ad dark phase

ad light phase

ad dark phase
moulting

juv

juv

imm

imm

ad ♂ breeding

POMARINE SKUA

juv

juv

ad

LONG-TAILED SKUA

imm moulting

juv

ad
non-breeding

ad breeding

Plate 53

SKUAS and GULLS

BROWN SKUA (Hakoakoa) *Catharacta skua*

Locally common native

63 cm; ♂ 1675 g, ♀ 1950 g. Very large stocky skua, like a large juvenile Black-backed Gull but *chocolate brown* except for some variable bronzy-yellow flecking on hindneck and *conspicuous white flashes on wings*. Wings broad and rounded; large hooked black bill; legs and feet black. Juvenile lacks yellow on hindneck, often more mottled and rusty on upperparts. In flight, slow powerful wingbeats and short glides. On breeding grounds, defends territory with raucous calls and low dives. **Habitat:** Breeds circumpolar subantarctic; in NZ region, on Chathams, Fiordland coast, islands around Stewart I, Solanders, The Snares, Antipodes, Auckland and Campbell Is, especially near seabird colonies. Disperse through southern oceans; occasionally seen on NZ mainland in winter, often at beach-washed offal. **Breeding:** Sep–Feb.

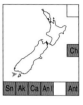

SOUTH POLAR SKUA *Catharacta maccormicki*

Locally common native

59 cm; ♂ 1275 g, ♀ 1425 g. Large stocky skua, like Brown Skua but smaller; *shorter stubbier black bill*; more yellow feathering on hindneck. Variable plumages from pale to all dark, but all have *prominent white wing flashes*. Wings broad and rounded; tail short; legs and feet black. Pale phase has head and underparts pale ashy grey-brown with yellowish collar and brown back, wings and tail. Dark phase has body brown; back, wings and tail paler brown; white flecks at base of bill; buff collar. Juvenile lacks collar and has pale feather edges on upperparts, giving a scaly appearance. **Habitat:** Breeds Antarctica, including Ross Sea, usually near seabird colonies. Occasionally beach-wrecked or seen off coast of NZ mainland while on passage to N Pacific, usually Jan–Apr. **Breeding:** Nov–Mar.

Gulls, terns and noddies are a large cosmopolitan group of mainly coastal birds. Most have short straight bills and short legs. Sexes alike. Usually grey, black or brown above, and white below in adults; juveniles usually have brown barring on back and wings. Bill and legs are often brightly coloured but usually change with age and/or season.

BLACK-BACKED GULL (Karoro) *Larus dominicanus*

Abundant native

60 cm; ♂ 1050 g, ♀ 850 g. The only large gull in NZ. Languid shallow wingbeats interspersed with long glides separate it from distant skuas and mollymawks. Juvenile dull brown, pale feather edges give a mottled appearance, especially on head, neck and underparts; bill and eye dark brown; legs pinkish brown. In flight, looks dark brown with a paler rump. 2nd year has head, neck and underparts white, mottled and flecked brown; back and upperwings scruffy brown and black; bill dull yellowish or greenish, darker at tip; legs pinkish brown to greyish green. In flight, rump white, mottled brown, tail usually barred brown and white, wings darker towards tips. 3rd year has head and underparts white; neck lightly flecked brown; back and upperwings brown and black, the extent of black depending on the stage of moult; rump and tail white, with black band across tip. Bill dull yellow, darker at tip; legs yellowish green. Adult has head, neck, underparts, rump and tail white, back and upperwings black with narrow white trailing edge; bill yellow with red spot at tip of lower bill; eye pale yellow; legs greenish yellow. **Habitat:** Breeds circumpolar subantarctic; in NZ region, on coast of mainland, offshore and outlying islands, except only straggles to Kermadecs and The Snares; also breeds far inland on riverbeds, near lakes and alpine tarns. Ranges widely, feeds at rubbish tips, farmland, ploughed fields, beaches, harbours and behind boats, but rarely ventures far out to sea. **Breeding:** Oct–Feb.

BROWN SKUA

SOUTH POLAR SKUA

dark phase

pale phase

pale phase

Black-backed Gull
juv

ad

juv

3rd year

2nd year

BLACK-BACKED GULL   ad

Plate 54

GULLS and TERNS

RED-BILLED GULL (Tarapunga) *Larus novaehollandiae*   **Abundant native**

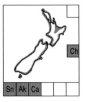

37 cm; ♂ 300 g, ♀ 260 g. Grey and white gull, mainly of the coast. Like Black-billed Gull but *shorter deeper bill* and boldly patterned wingtips. Adult has head, underparts and tail white, sometimes pinkish on breast; back and *wings pearly grey, except wingtips black with small white window*. Short deep bright red bill; legs and feet red; eye brown. Juvenile and 1st year have larger dark patch at wingtip and very small, if any, white window. Bill dark with pink near base; legs pale flesh to reddish black; eye brown. **Habitat:** Breeds subantarctic from Africa to Chathams; in NZ region, on coast from Three Kings to Campbell Is; inland colony at Lake Rotorua. Common in coastal waters, beaches and estuaries; only occasionally (but sometimes in large flocks) inland to wet paddocks, playing fields and lakes. **Breeding:** Oct–Feb.

BLACK-BILLED GULL *Larus bulleri*   **Common endemic**

37 cm; ♂ 300 g, ♀ 250 g. *Very pale* gull of inland South I and coasts. Like Red-billed Gull but *longer thinner bill* and very pale wingtips. Adult has back and *wings pale silvery grey, wingtips only thinly bordered black*. Long thin black bill; legs and feet black or reddish black; eye white. Juvenile quickly loses small grey patch behind eye; has more extensive black on wingtips; bill pale flesh with dark tip; legs from pinkish to reddish black; eye brown. **Habitat:** Breeds on riverbeds and lake margins of South I, some also in southern North I and at Lake Rotorua; a few coastal colonies in both islands. Feeds inland in wet paddocks, ploughed fields and over lakes; also coastal waters, beaches and estuaries. **Breeding:** Sep–Feb.

CASPIAN TERN (Taranui) *Sterna caspia*   **Uncommon native**

51 cm, 700 g. *Very large silver-grey tern with massive red bill* tipped black and yellow; short white, slightly forked tail; underparts white with dark tips to underwing. Adult has black cap when breeding, heavily flecked white in non-breeding plumage; legs black. Juvenile has browner cap; back feathers sparsely edged buff and white; bill orange-red; legs dull orange. Flight direct, with steady shallow beats of broad wings; head and bill pointing downward when hunting. Dives into water. Adult call a loud harsh 'kaaa'; juveniles beg with a persistent high-pitched mewing. **Habitat:** Breeds widely; in NZ, colonies on isolated sandspits and shellbanks of coast and harbours; some pairs on riverbeds or lake shores. Feeds in inshore waters, up rivers and over coastal lakes. Vagrant to Kermadecs and Chathams. **Breeding:** Sep–Jan.

CRESTED TERN *Sterna bergii*   **Rare tropical vagrant**

47 cm, 350 g. *Large tern with long slender greenish-yellow bill*. Breeding adult has white forehead, black cap and a *straggly crest*; upperparts *slate grey*, paler on rump and tail; underparts white; legs black. Non-breeding adult has crown white or streaked black. Juvenile similar, but cap browner and extends around eye, wings brownish grey and mottled. Looks rakish yet graceful in flight. Plunge-dives. Noisy; call a rasping 'kerrcrik'. **Habitat:** Breeds eastern Asia, S Pacific and Australia. A few reach NZ coasts.

GULL-BILLED TERN *Gelochelidon nilotica*   **Rare subtropical vagrant**

43 cm, 230 g. *Robust pale tern with long broad wings, short slightly forked tail, short thick gull-like black bill and long black legs*. Breeding adult has black cap; back and wings very pale grey; neck and underparts white. Non-breeding adult has a *black patch from eye to ear coverts*, and grey flecking on nape. Hawks and skims over water or land, picking up prey in flight; rarely dives into water. **Habitat:** Breeds tropics and subtropics, including Australia. A few reach NZ estuaries and coastal marshes.

RED-BILLED GULL

juv

juv

BLACK-BILLED GULL

juv

juv

CASPIAN TERN

juv

non-breeding

breeding

CRESTED TERN

juv

non-breeding

breeding

Crested Tern
juv

non-breeding

breeding

GULL-BILLED TERN

Plate 55

TERNS

WHITE-FRONTED TERN (Tara) *Sterna striata*   Abundant native

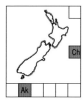

40 cm, 160 g. Commonest tern on NZ coast, often in large flocks. *Long black bill*; short legs, black or reddish black. Breeding adult is very pale pearly grey and white; *black cap separated from bill by white forehead*; neck and underparts white, sometimes pinkish on breast. In flight, *upperwing entirely pale grey* except for black outer web to outer primary; *underwing white to tips*. At rest, deeply forked tail extends well beyond wings. Non-breeding adult similar, but cap recedes to above eyes; at rest, tail level with wings. Juvenile heavily marked brown and white on upperparts; dark mottling on upperwing (carpal bar), prominent at rest, and in flight forms a dark triangle on inner forewing; primaries mid-grey; tail even with or shorter than wings. Immature similar, but mottling on inner forewing shows as black line at shoulder. Feeds by plunge-diving. Call a high-pitched 'siet'. **Habitat:** Breeds coast of NZ mainland, Chatham and Auckland Is; visitor to other subantarctic islands. Favours coastal waters and harbours. Large flocks form over shoaling fish, especially in summer and autumn. Roosts on shellbanks or sandspits. Rarely seen inland. Many, including most juveniles, winter in Australian waters. **Breeding:** Oct–Feb.

COMMON TERN *Sterna hirundo*   Rare Arctic migrant

36 cm, 120 g. Like small dark White-fronted Tern, but bill shorter and finer; legs rather long. At rest, deeply forked tail even with or slightly shorter than wings. Breeding adult has black cap *sloping* down to black bill with dull red base; pearl-grey underparts. In flight, *outermost 3–4 dark grey primaries contrast with paler grey inner primaries*, which appear as a *translucent patch* against the light, diffuse trailing edge to tip of underwings; dark outer edge to tail; reddish-black legs. In non-breeding plumage, black cap recedes to level of eye; underparts white; many have prominent carpal bar at rest; bill black; legs reddish black. Immature similar, but primaries darker, and tertials often have brownish tips. Flight more buoyant than White-fronted Tern, wingbeats faster and deeper. Feeds by plunge-diving; frequently hovers. Calls a short 'kik' and a raspy 'kreer'. **Habitat:** Breeds subarctic. Migrates to temperate oceans. Only a few identified in NZ, mainly from North I coasts or coastal lakes.

ARCTIC TERN *Sterna paradisaea*   Rare Arctic migrant

34 cm, 110 g. Like small dark White-fronted Tern and similar to Common Tern, but paler, smaller-bodied and longer-winged. Head rounded except *steep forehead*; bill rather short; *legs very short, brilliant red to reddish black*. Breeding adult has black cap down to blood-red bill; underparts darker grey than upperparts; small amount of black on tips of outer 3–4 primaries; *all of outerwing appears translucent* against the light except for a *thin well-defined dark trailing edge to tip of underwing*; thin dark outer edge to tail; at rest, deeply forked tail even with or longer than wings; red legs. In non-breeding plumage, cap recedes to *behind eye*; underparts white; some develop a faint carpal bar; bill black. Immature has thin carpal bar and darker primaries. In flight, looks slim, long-winged and long-tailed. Flight buoyant, with deeper, faster wingbeats than White-fronted Tern. Calls like Common Tern. **Habitat:** Breeds Arctic. Migrates to southern oceans. A few seen each summer at NZ estuaries or coastal lakes.

ANTARCTIC TERN *Sterna vittata*   Locally common native

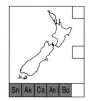

36 cm, 140 g. Medium-sized tern with white rump and forked tail. Breeding adult has black cap down to red bill; white cheeks; even grey body; wings grey with black only on the outer web of the outer primary; legs red. Non-breeding adult similar, but cap recedes to just behind eye; underparts white; bill dull pinkish red. Juvenile initially marked brown and white on back; bill dark brown, legs dull reddish. In flight, thinner-winged and more delicate than White-fronted Tern, and wings lack dark markings. Feeds by dipping and plunge-diving. **Habitat:** Breeds circumpolar subantarctic, including NZ subantarctic south of Stewart I. Stays close to breeding sites and not recorded off mainland. **Breeding:** Sep–Apr.

WHITE-FRONTED TERN

imm

non-breeding

ad

imm

breeding

juv

imm

ad Common

non-breeding

breeding

imm Common

COMMON TERN

imm

imm Arctic

non-breeding

breeding

ad Arctic

ARCTIC TERN

imm

non-breeding

ad

ANTARCTIC TERN

breeding

juv

Plate 56

TERNS

BLACK-FRONTED TERN (Tarapiroe)   *Sterna albostriata*   **Common endemic**

29 cm, 80 g. The common inland tern of the South I. Smaller and greyer than White-fronted Tern. *Blue-grey body, wings and short shallow-forked tail contrasts with white rump* in flight; undertail white; *bill and legs orange.* Breeding adult has black cap down to bill; thin white streak across cheeks; *bill and legs bright orange.* Non-breeding adult similar, but cap recedes to arc from eye to eye around back of head, except crown flecked grey; bill and legs dull orange. Immature has crown flecked black; dark patches around eye; chin white; breast very pale grey; bill dusky brown, becoming yellow with age; legs dull orange. Feeds mainly by hawking insects over riverbeds and dropping to pick prey from the surface of lakes, swamps and farmland. **Habitat:** Breeds in small colonies on gravel riverbeds of South I, mainly east of Alps. Migrates to coast to feed at sea, especially in Cook Strait and off eastern coast of North and South Is, as far north as Bay of Plenty. **Breeding:** Oct–Feb.

WHITE-WINGED BLACK TERN   *Chlidonias leucopterus*   **Uncommon Asian migrant**

23 cm, 65 g. Distinctive very small tern with slow buoyant flight. Black and white in breeding plumage; grey and white in non-breeding, but with distinctive *black 'ear-muffs' and club-shaped patch on nape.* Breeding adult has black head, neck, back and underparts: white rump and only barely forked tail; upperwing very pale grey, darker at tips; underwing black at base, white at tips; bill and legs red. Non-breeding adult has white head except crown streaked black, and black club-shaped band extends over top of head from behind eyes and also down nape; grey back; upperwing grey, darker at tips and along trailing edge of secondaries; shows dark carpal bar at rest; rump, tail and underparts white; bill and legs black, some with reddish tinge. Immature similar, but upperwings darker grey, rump very pale grey and tail grey. Hawks insects over water or land; flies persistently back and forth, dropping down to pick insects from water surface; rarely plunges. **Habitat:** Breeds Eurasia. Migrates to tropics and subtropics. A few reach NZ coastal lakes, swamps and estuaries each year.

WHISKERED TERN   *Chlidonias hybrida*   **Rare Australian vagrant**

26 cm, 90 g. Small tern with slow buoyant flight, long legs and gull-like stance; *even grey on rump and slightly forked tail.* Breeding adult has black cap down to red bill; white cheeks; dark grey underparts and sooty belly contrasts with white undertail; red legs. Non-breeding is pale grey above and dull white below with black arc from eye to eye around back of head, solid on ears but flecked on nape; wingtips darker than rest of wings; bill and legs dull red-brown. Immature similar but narrow dark borders to upperwing, and rump slightly paler than rest of upperparts. Feeds by hawking insects, picking prey from the water surface or by taking shallow plunges into water. **Habitat:** Breeds Africa to Australia; nomadic or migratory. A few reach NZ, mainly at coastal lakes or sewage ponds.

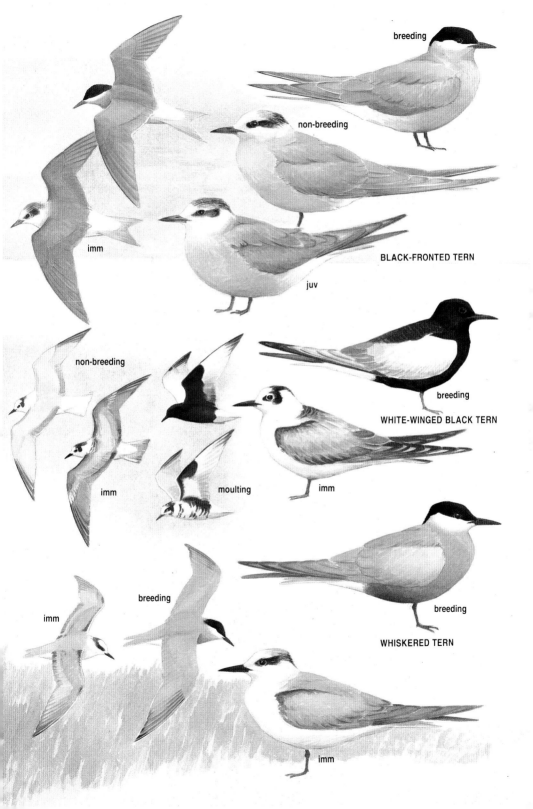

breeding

non-breeding

imm

juv

BLACK-FRONTED TERN

non-breeding

imm

moulting

imm

breeding

WHITE-WINGED BLACK TERN

breeding

WHISKERED TERN

imm

breeding

imm

Plate 57
TERNS

LITTLE TERN   *Sterna albifrons*
Uncommon Asian migrant

25 cm, 50 g. Very small vocal tern; very like dark Fairy Tern, but *dark primaries contrast with rest of upperwing.* Flight erratic with rapid deep wingbeats, often hovers. Breeding adult has white *sloping forehead* and *sharp recess to just behind eye*; black crown, nape and *line through eye to yellow bill with black tip*; upperparts pale grey, darker on wingtips with outermost 2–3 primaries black; deeply forked white tail; underparts white; legs orange-yellow. In non-breeding plumage (seen in NZ summer), cap recedes to band from eye to eye around back of head and down nape; bill dull yellow, dusky at tip; legs dull yellow. Immature similar, but bill black and *dark leading edge to wing* prominent as dark shoulder (carpal) bar at rest; some retain brown feather tips on upperparts; legs blackish brown. Flight call a sharp chattering 'kik, kik, kik . . .' and a rasping 'kree-ik'. **Habitat:** Breeds widely in Northern Hemisphere and Australia. Most in NZ are in non-breeding plumage in Oct–Mar, probably migrants from E Asia. Single birds and small flocks regularly seen at NZ estuaries or coastal lakes, mainly at North I harbours, especially Firth of Thames.

FAIRY TERN   *Sterna nereis*
Rare native

25 cm, 70 g. Very small tern, very like pale Little Tern but *upperwing almost uniform pale grey.* Flight erratic with rapid deep wingbeats; often hovers. Breeding adult (Oct–Mar) has white *steep forehead* and *rounded recess to above eye*; black crown, nape and *line to eye; white feathering between eye and pure yellow-orange bill*; upperparts uniform pale grey; deeply forked white tail; underparts white; legs orange-yellow. In non-breeding plumage, cap recedes to above eye and down nape; bill orange-brown, dusky at tip and base; legs dull orange. Immature similar, but bill black with dusky-yellow base, thin *dark leading edge to wing* faintly visible as dark shoulder (carpal) bar at rest; legs brown. Flight call a high-pitched 'zwit'. **Habitat:** Breeds Australia, New Caledonia and NZ. The NZ subspecies, which is endangered, breeds on a few Northland sandspits, and feeds on nearby estuaries, especially Kaipara Harbour in winter. **Breeding:** Nov–Feb.

GREY TERNLET   *Procelsterna cerulea*
Locally common native

28 cm, 75 g. Distinctive small delicate *blue-grey tern. Wings darker grey, especially at tips, and with a thin white trailing edge.* Prominent eye owing to small black patch in front of eye; long forked tail; bill black; long black legs, feet black with yellow to pink webs. Juvenile has head streaked and upperparts and wings washed brownish. Flight graceful. Feeds by hovering, fluttering and paddling on sea surface like a huge Storm Petrel; sometimes settles on the surface. **Habitat:** Tropical and subtropical Pacific; in NZ region, breeds at Kermadecs, in some years also at Three Kings Is and rock stacks off eastern coast of Northland and in Bay of Plenty. Occasionally seen in northern NZ coastal waters; straggles as far south as Canterbury. **Breeding:** Aug–Feb.

WHITE TERN   *Gygis alba*
Rare native

31 cm, 110 g. *Delicate pure white tern* with almost translucent wings and short forked tail; prominent eye owing to narrow black ring of feathers around eye; long straight bill, black with bluish base; legs and feet blue-grey with yellowish webs. Juvenile has smudgy brown patch behind eye and across back of head, and rusty brown flecks on back and upperwings. Flight swift and graceful; often circles over breeding areas by day. **Habitat:** Tropical seas; in NZ, breeds at Kermadecs, vagrants occasionally reach NZ mainland. **Breeding:** Oct–Mar.

LITTLE TERN

breeding

non-breeding

imm

imm

FAIRY TERN

breeding

non-breeding

imm

imm

GREY TERNLET

WHITE TERN

Plate 58

TERNS and NODDIES

SOOTY TERN   *Sterna fuscata*   Locally common native

45 cm, 210 g. Large tropical tern. Adult has white forehead and eyebrow to just above eye; cap, line through eye to bill, nape and *upperparts dark brownish black*; sides of neck and underparts white, washed pale grey towards long deeply forked tail. Bill and legs black. Juvenile dark brown except feathers on back and upperwings edged white or buff, underwings pale grey, and underparts white towards tail. Distinctive harsh 'wideawake' call. **Habitat:** Breeds tropics and subtropics, including Kermadecs. After breeding, ranges widely over deep water and a few reach northern NZ, especially after autumn and winter gales. **Breeding:** Oct–Mar.

BRIDLED TERN   *Sterna anaethetus*   Rare tropical vagrant

41 cm, 120 g. Like small pale Sooty Tern. Adult has white forehead and eyebrow extending well behind eye; black cap, line through eye to bill, and nape contrasts with dark grey-brown upperparts; sides of neck and underparts white, long deeply forked tail. Bill and legs black. Juvenile similar, but crown streaked white, incomplete black line between eye and bill, and feathers on back and upperwings edged white or buff. **Habitat:** Breeds tropics, including northern Australia. One NZ record: Canterbury, November 1987.

COMMON NODDY   *Anous stolidus*   Rare native

39 cm, 200 g. Medium-sized dark tropical tern with *very long broad tail* with shallow central notch. Like large White-capped Noddy but *browner*, and in flight, *underwing has pale central panel*. Adult has whitish-grey forehead and cap, merging into brown on sides of face and nape; black line from bill to eye; body, upperwing and tail dark brown; underwing grey-brown, edged dark brown. Thin straight (4.5 cm) black bill; legs and feet black. Juvenile similar but duller, cap less clearly defined, and back and wing feathers edged pale. Flight buoyant. Feeds mainly from sea surface and sometimes settles on the water. **Habitat:** Tropics and subtropics; recently found breeding on Curtis I, Kermadecs. After breeding, disperses to feed in flocks over deep warm waters. Three records from near the NZ mainland. **Breeding:** Sep–Jan.

WHITE-CAPPED (Lesser) NODDY   *Anous tenuirostris*   Locally common native

37 cm, 100 g. Medium-sized dark tropical tern with long broad tail, square or slightly notched. Like small Common Noddy but *blacker, and in flight has completely dark underwings*. Adult has silvery-white forehead, cap to level of eyes, and hindcrown; black line from bill to eye; sooty black neck, body and wings; tail brownish black, underwings black. Fine slightly decurved (4 cm) black bill; legs and feet dark brown. Juvenile similar but less white on hindcrown, sharper separation of pale crown from dark neck, and feathers on back and wings edged pale. Flight buoyant; feeds mainly from sea surface but sometimes dives; occasionally settles on the water. **Habitat:** Breeds tropics and subtropics, including Kermadecs. After breeding, remains close to breeding sites, but vagrants occasionally reach NZ mainland, mostly in autumn after northerly gales. **Breeding:** Aug–Apr.

SOOTY TERN

juv

juv

BRIDLED TERN

juv

COMMON NODDY

WHITE-CAPPED NODDY

Plate 59

PIGEONS and DOVES

Medium to large landbirds with short bill, small head, rounded wings and short feathered legs. Sexes alike. Calls simple and often repetitive variations of 'coo'. Flight strong, direct and often noisy. Aerial displays of stall dives are part of breeding displays. Can breed at any time of year if food supplies are suitable. Lay 1–2 white eggs on a flimsy platform of sticks. Short incubation and nestling periods; young fed 'crop milk' and, later, other regurgitated food. They often fledge well below adult weight, with short wings and tail, and dull bill and feet. All are herbivorous; the New Zealand Pigeon feeds on fruit and foliage, the three introduced species feed on seeds, especially grain.

NEW ZEALAND PIGEON (Kereru, Kukupa, Parea) *Hemiphaga novaeseelandiae*
Common endemic

51 cm, 650 g (mainland); 55 cm, 800 g (Chathams). Largest pigeon in NZ. Head, throat, upper breast and upperparts metallic green with purplish sheen and bronze reflections, especially around neck (mainland), or with ashy-grey wash (Chathams); sharp line separates upper breast from white lower breast, belly and legs. Eye crimson; bill red with orangish tip; feet crimson. Juvenile similar, but upperparts duller, smudgy upper breast, dull bill and feet, and often the tail is shorter. In flight, strong steady wingbeats, broad rounded wings and long broad tail; *noisy swish of wings* is distinctive. Call a single soft penetrating 'kuu'. **Habitat:** Native forests, especially in lowland areas, scrub, forest patches among farmland, rural and city gardens and parks. **Breeding:** Variable, depending on availability of ripe fruit; usually Oct–Apr.

ROCK (Feral) PIGEON *Columba livia*
Common European introduction

33 cm, 400 g. Highly variable plumages seen in descendants of domestic and racing pigeons. In the wild form, the plumage is mainly blue-grey, with sides of neck glossy green and purple; rump whitish; two prominent black bars across the wings; dark tip to the tail. Bill leaden; feet pinkish. Flight fast and direct, with flicking wingbeats; pointed angled wings, and short tail. **Habitat:** City parks and streets; grain stores, wharfs and railway stations. In rural areas, favours drier arable farmland. Often nests on cliffs and caves in river gorges and on sea coast. **Breeding:** All year, peak Sep–Feb.

BARBARY DOVE *Streptopelia roseogrisea*
Rare African introduction

28 cm, 140 g. *Pale creamy buff*, shading to white on chin, belly and undertail coverts; distinctive *black half-collar* around back of neck. Eye red; bill horn-black; feet crimson. Juvenile similar but lacks black half-collar and has pale bill. Distinctive call: a *persistent 'coo-crooo'*. **Habitat:** Parks, gardens and orchards in South Auckland and near Whangarei, Rotorua, Whakatane and Havelock North. **Breeding:** Oct–Feb.

SPOTTED DOVE *Streptopelia chinensis*
Uncommon Asian introduction

30 cm, 130 g. Head grey, tinged pink; *nape and back of neck black, finely spotted with white*; back, wings and rump mottled brown; tail long, with darker outer feathers, broadly tipped with white. Eye red; bill black; feet pink. Juvenile similar but lacks patterning on nape. Calls mellow, varying from 1 to 4 notes: 'coo', 'croo-croo', 'coo-coo-croo', 'coo-coo-croo-coor'. **Habitat:** Suburban parks, gardens, farmland and orchards of Auckland, South Auckland, and near Te Puke and Opotiki. **Breeding:** Oct–Feb.

Chatham Island

NEW ZEALAND PIGEON

ROCK PIGEON

BARBARY DOVE

juv

SPOTTED DOVE

Plate 60

PARROTS

A large cosmopolitan family of often very colourful birds, but the NZ species are relatively drab, mainly green. All have a short bill with a horn covering (cere) enclosing the nostrils. The upper mandible is strongly curved, fitting neatly over the lower mandible. Their legs are short, and their feet have two toes pointing forward and two back.

SULPHUR-CRESTED COCKATOO   *Cacatua galerita*
Uncommon Australian introduction

50 cm, 900 g. A large *white parrot with a bright yellow crest*; a yellow tinge on underwing and undertail; bill and legs grey-black. Female slightly larger. Flies strongly on broad rounded wings, screeching raucously. Often feeds on the ground. **Habitat:** Forest patches in open country, especially western Waikato and Turakina River. **Breeding:** Aug–Jan.

KAKAPO   *Strigops habroptilus*
Rare endemic

63 cm; ♂ 2.5 kg, ♀ 2 kg. Large flightless nocturnal parrot. *Moss green above, greenish yellow below*; feathers mottled with fine brown and yellow bars. Owl-like facial disc. Male has broader head and larger bill. Feeds on ground or by clambering into shrubs. Male call a *loud repetitive booming* for hours, from cleared track-and-bowl system on ridge of prominent hill. **Habitat:** Formerly in forests of three main islands; introduced and now confined to Little Barrier, Maud and Codfish Is, unless a few persist in Fiordland. **Breeding:** Usually every 3–5 years, Dec–Jul.

KEA   *Nestor notabilis*
Locally common endemic

46 cm; ♂ 1000 g, ♀ 800 g. A large, often bold parrot, olive green with scarlet underwings and rump. Dark-edged feathers make it look sculpted. Bill, cere, eye and legs dark brown; upper mandible longer in the male. Juvenile has pale crown, yellow cere, eye-ring and on bill; yellow fades in a couple of years to bill only. *Call a loud ringing 'keee-aa'*, mainly in flight. Delights in aerobatics and playful but sometimes destructive behaviour. **Habitat:** Mainly in alpine zone, but also in forest and descends to lowland river flats. **Breeding:** Jul–Mar.

KAKA   *Nestor meridionalis*
Locally common endemic

45 cm; ♂ 525 g, ♀ 475 g. A large sometimes inquisitive *forest parrot* with crimson underwings and rump. North I birds are mainly olive brown with darker feather edges; crown paler and greyer; golden wash on cheeks; dark crimson collar, undertail and lower belly. Bill longer and more arched in the male. Juvenile has yellow base of lower mandible. South and Stewart Is birds (illustrated) brighter, and crown almost white. Noisy; many varied calls from liquid whistling notes to harsh grating calls. **Habitat:** Favours native forest and predator- and possum-free offshore islands, but a few visit gardens and orchards. **Breeding:** Sep–Apr.

GALAH   *Cacatua roseicapilla*
Rare Australian introduction

36 cm, 325 g. A noisy *pink and grey parrot* with paler crown and crest. Immature duller than adult, with grey about the face. **Habitat:** Forest patches in open country; recently established in South Auckland, especially near Hunua Ranges, Pukekohe, and Pakihi and Ponui Is. **Breeding:** Season unknown in NZ.

SULPHUR-CRESTED COCKATOO

KAKAPO

KEA

KAKA

GALAH

Plate 61

PARROTS

CRIMSON ROSELLA *Platycercus elegans* Rare Australian introduction

35 cm, 130 g. Distinctive medium-sized parrot with a long tail. Adult *rich crimson with blue cheeks*, wings and tail, mottled black on the back. Immature green but with crimson on forehead, breast and undertail, blue on chin, wings and tail. **Habitat:** Parks and gardens in Wellington. **Breeding:** Sep–Feb.

EASTERN ROSELLA *Platycercus eximius* Locally common Australian introduction

32 cm, 110 g. Distinctive long-tailed parrot with a bell-like *'kwink, kwink' flight call.* Head, upper breast and undertail crimson; *cheeks white*; lower breast yellow; back, rump, flanks and belly yellowish green, mottled black on back; leading edge of inner wing black, contrasts with pale blue on the central wing and dark blue on the wingtips; tail dark bluish green, edged pale blue. Female and immature more heavily mottled black on back, and red areas duller and patchy. Loud ringing calls and chattering notes. **Habitat:** Favours lightly wooded country (e.g. scattered totara) but uses forest and urban parks and gardens. **Breeding:** Oct–Jan.

YELLOW-CROWNED PARAKEET (Kakariki) *Cyanoramphus auriceps*
Locally common endemic

♂ 25 cm, 50 g; ♀ 23 cm, 40 g. Long-tailed bright yellow-green parrot of native forest. *Crown golden yellow*; forehead and band from bill *to* eye red, and small patch on sides of rump crimson; violet-blue on wing coverts and some outer flight feathers. Orange-fronted colour phase is plainer green, lacking yellow; forehead and band from bill to eye orange. Flight fast and direct, with rapid wingbeats. *Flight call a rapid high-pitched chatter.* **Habitat:** Native forests; rare orange-fronted phase is seen mostly in North Canterbury. **Breeding:** Oct–Feb.

RED-CROWNED PARAKEET (Kakariki) *Cyanoramphus novaezelandiae*
Locally common native

♂ 28 cm, 80 g; ♀ 25 cm, 70 g. Very like the Yellow-crowned Parakeet but larger and with red crown, forehead and band from bill to *behind* eye; rump patches crimson. Flight direct and rapid, often above the canopy, or side-slipping through the trees. *Flight call a rapid loud chatter*, lower-pitched than Yellow-crowned Parakeet. **Habitat:** Rare in native forests on the main islands but common in forest and scrub on Stewart I and many predator-free offshore and outlying islands. **Breeding:** Oct–Mar.

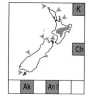

ANTIPODES ISLAND PARAKEET *Cyanoramphus unicolor*
Locally common endemic

♂ 32 cm, ♀ 29 cm; 130 g. Visibly larger and plumper than other NZ parakeets. *Entirely green head* and body, except for blue on wing coverts and some flight feathers; underparts tinged yellow. **Habitat:** Tussock and scrub of Antipodes Is only. **Breeding:** Oct–Mar.

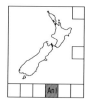

CRIMSON ROSELLA

juv

EASTERN
ROSELLA

♂

♀

YELLOW-CROWNED
PARAKEET

orange-fronted
phase

RED-CROWNED
PARAKEET

ANTIPODES ISLAND
PARAKEET

Plate 62

CUCKOOS

A diverse group ranging in size from the Shining Cuckoo to the Channel-billed Cuckoo. Generally grey or brown, often with conspicuous barring, especially on the underparts; long tail with transverse bars and white notches; short bill and short legs. Sexes alike. Most lay 1 egg in nests of other insectivorous species. Young cuckoos make insistent penetrating begging calls. The adults are vocal when breeding and are more often heard than seen.

SHINING CUCKOO (Pipiwharauroa) *Chrysococcyx lucidus* **Common native**

16 cm, 25 g. Short-tailed *metallic bronze-green cuckoo, barred dark green on white face and underparts.* Juvenile duller and less distinctly barred. Song a distinctive *series of high-pitched upward-slurring whistles: 'coo-ee, coo-ee . . .' followed by 1–2 downward-slurring notes: 'tsee-ew'*; the latter often given when flying at night. Usual host is Grey Warbler. **Habitat:** Native forest, scrub, parks and gardens from Sep–Apr. Migrates to Solomon Is and Bismark Archipelago for NZ winter. **Breeding:** Oct–Feb.

LONG-TAILED CUCKOO (Koekoea) *Eudynamys taitensis* **Locally common endemic**

40 cm, 125 g. Large *brown cuckoo with very long tail.* Adult has upperparts rich brown, barred black; face and underparts pale buff, boldly streaked brown and black. Juvenile has upperparts dull brown, spotted white; face and underparts buff, lightly streaked. Main call a loud harsh shriek – 'zzwheesht' – from a high perch or in flight, any time of day. In flight, tail as long as body. Usual hosts are Whitehead, Brown Creeper and Yellowhead. **Habitat:** Mainly native and exotic forest, Oct–Mar, but almost anywhere on migration. Migrates to Pacific islands. **Breeding:** Nov–Jan.

CHANNEL-BILLED CUCKOO *Scythrops novaehollandiae* **Rare Australian vagrant**

61 cm. Huge grey cuckoo with a long black and white-tipped tail, and large powerful yellow bill. Red skin round the red eye. **Habitat:** Breeds Australian forests. Winters in Indonesia. Rarely seen in NZ, spring and summer.

PALLID CUCKOO *Cuculus pallidus* **Rare Australian vagrant**

30 cm, 85 g. Medium-sized cuckoo with long wings and tail and falcon-like profile in flight. Adult plain grey, barred only on undertail; a dark grey line passes through the eye; pale eyebrow and patch on the nape. Immature boldly marked brown and buff on head and upperparts; pale buff underparts. Feeds by swooping to ground from a perch. Male song a series of *slowly rising and accelerating melancholy notes: 'too, too . . . too, too'*. **Habitat:** Breeds Australia. Winters northern Australia, New Guinea and Indonesia. A few reach NZ, mainly in lightly forested open country.

ORIENTAL CUCKOO *Cuculus saturatus* **Rare Asian straggler**

33 cm. Like large Pallid Cuckoo but darker grey, and *lower chest, belly and undertail boldly barred black on white*. Rare brown phase rich brown above, paler below and heavily barred black all over. Feeds by swooping to ground from a perch. Usually silent in NZ. **Habitat:** Breeds Asia. Migrates to Indonesia and Australia. A few reach NZ, mainly in lightly forested open country.

FAN-TAILED CUCKOO *Cacomantis flabelliformis* **Rare Australian vagrant**

26 cm. Slim cuckoo with habit of cocking and fanning tail on alighting on a perch. Adult *blue-grey above, mostly rust red below, but with tail notched black on white*. Immature speckled rufous and brown with pale brown belly and undertail coverts, dark bars on chest and undertail. Feeds by swooping to ground from a perch. Call a repeated rapid descending trill. **Habitat:** Breeds Australia and SW Pacific. Vagrants reach NZ, mainly in lightly forested open country.

SHINING CUCKOO

CHANNEL-BILLED
CUCKOO

juv

LONG-TAILED CUCKOO

FAN-TAILED
CUCKOO

PALLID CUCKOO

ORIENTAL
CUCKOO

juv

brown phase

Plate 63

OWLS and KINGFISHERS

Owls are mainly nocturnal birds of prey. They are chunky, and usually streaked brown and buff and spotted white. Large head and flat-faced with large eyes in a paler facial disc. Bill short and hooked. Powerful feet and talons. Sexes alike; females slightly larger. Plumage is soft, and so flight is silent. Voice ranges from plaintive calls to harsh screeches.

LITTLE OWL *Athene noctua*   Locally common European introduction

23 cm, 180 g. *Small grey-brown owl, heavily streaked and spotted white.* Flatter head and shorter tail than Morepork. Often seen by day perching on posts and farm sheds. Flight undulating. Call a clear high-pitched 'kiew'. **Habitat:** Farmland of South I only, especially near east coast. **Breeding:** Oct–Jan.

MOREPORK (Ruru) *Ninox novaeseelandiae*   Common native

29 cm, 175 g. *Dark brown owl*, obscurely spotted and barred buff. Yellow eyes set in dark facial mask. Larger rounder head and longer tail than Little Owl. Nocturnal; roosts by day in thick vegetation, especially in tree ferns. Main call a loud double hoot – *'more-pork'* – also repeated monotonous 'more' and rising vibrating 'cree'. **Habitat:** Forest, scrub, lightly forested open country, parks and gardens. **Breeding:** Sep–Mar.

BARN OWL *Tyto alba*   Rare Australian vagrant

34 cm. *Large pale buff and white owl*; looks white when seen at dusk or in headlights. Heart-shaped white facial disc. Call a rasping screech: 'skiirrr'. **Habitat:** Almost worldwide in open country.

Kingfishers are small to large birds with a dumpy body, short neck, short legs, large head, and a bill that looks too large and heavy. Sexes alike. Often but not always associated with water. They sit patiently on a branch, powerline or other prominent perch and dart or glide to snatch prey from the ground surface, or to plunge into shallow water. Calls are harsh.

KOOKABURRA *Dacelo novaeguineae*   Rare Australian introduction

45 cm, 350 g. *Very large bird with heavy black and yellow bill*; pale head and underparts, brownish back; tail rufous, barred black. Perches prominently on bare branch or powerline. In flight, clear white wing flashes. Voice a *raucous laughing cackle*, mainly at dawn and dusk. **Habitat:** Lightly forested open country, mainly from Orewa and Kaukapakapa to Whangarei, especially south of Wellsford. **Breeding:** Nov–Mar.

KINGFISHER (Kotare) *Halcyon sancta*   Abundant native

24 cm, 65 g. *Small deep green-blue and buff bird*; green grading to blue on the head and upperparts. Pale yellowish-buff to off-white underparts and collar round back of neck. Immature duller with buff feather edges on upperparts and brownish mottling on chest. Often seen *perched on powerlines, or on branches and rocks near water*. Call a *loud penetrating 'kek-kek-kek-kek'*. **Habitat:** Forest, river margins, farmland, lakes, estuaries and rocky coastlines; movement towards the coast in winter. **Breeding:** Oct–Feb.

MOREPORK

LITTLE OWL

BARN OWL

KOOKABURRA

KINGFISHER

imm

Plate 64

SWIFTS, SWALLOWS and MARTINS

Swifts are reminiscent of swallows but designed for aerial feeding and speed, with wide flattened bill and very long thin swept-back wings. Generally black, with white patches and distinctive tail shape. Sexes alike. They fly high, with bursts of rapid wingbeats alternating with long swift glides, dives and banking turns; at dusk and in bad weather, they fly low over water or circle headlands, hilltops and stands of tall trees. Rarely land (clinging to side of tree or building) except when breeding. Voice an excited twittering.

SPINE-TAILED SWIFT *Hirundapus caudacutus*   Rare tropical straggler

20 cm. Large swift with *short square tail*. All dark except for *white patches on throat and undertail*. In the hand, each tail feather has a short projecting spine. **Habitat:** Breeds E Asia. Migrates to Australia. Most stragglers to NZ seen over open country, mainly Nov–Mar.

FORK-TAILED SWIFT *Apus pacificus*   Rare tropical straggler

18 cm. Slightly smaller and slimmer than Spine-tailed Swift, with long *deeply-forked tail*. All dark except for *white rump and pale throat and lightly barred upperbreast*. **Habitat:** Breeds E Asia. Migrates to Australia. Stragglers to NZ seen over open country, mainly Oct–Feb, but some in winter.

Swallows and martins are small birds with rapid erratic darting and gliding flight in pursuit of flying insects or snatching them from the surface of water or the ground. NZ species mostly blue above, pale below; each species has distinctive combination of pattern of red on head, colour of rump, and shape of tail. Sexes alike. Juveniles duller. Perch and come to ground readily; often seen gathered on powerlines, fences, shed roofs and riverbed shingle. Build distinctive mud nests under bridges, in caves or rock outcrops, trees or around buildings. Lay 3–5 pale pink eggs, speckled brown.

WELCOME SWALLOW *Hirundo tahitica*   Abundant native

15 cm, 14 g. Adult has head and back blue-black; forehead, throat and chest rufous; underparts dull white; *deeply forked tail* with a row of white spots near the tip. Juvenile duller on upperparts, paler rufous markings, and tail less deeply forked. Often in swirling groups low over open water or crops, or sit on wires like clothes pegs. **Habitat:** Open country, especially near water. Often builds cup-shaped mud nest under bridges and under eaves of houses. **Breeding:** Aug–Mar.

AUSTRALIAN TREE MARTIN *Hirundo nigricans*   Rare Australian vagrant

13 cm. Smaller and stockier than Welcome Swallow. Head and back blue-black; forehead of adult rufous; juvenile pale rufous; underparts and *rump dull white; tail short, almost square*. **Habitat:** Vagrants regularly reach NZ in autumn and early winter, mainly in open country in company with Welcome Swallows.

FAIRY MARTIN *Hirundo ariel*   Rare Australian vagrant

12 cm. Much smaller than Welcome Swallow. *Whole head pale chestnut*; back blue-black; *rump bright white*; underparts dull white; *tail short, almost square*. **Habitat:** Rare vagrants reach NZ in Nov–Mar, mainly in open country. Distinctive bottle-shaped nest found in shed near Lake Wairarapa in 1970s.

SPINE-TAILED SWIFT

FORK-TAILED SWIFT

WELCOME SWALLOW

juv

juv

FAIRY MARTIN

AUSTRALIAN
TREE MARTIN

Plate 65

AUSTRALIAN PASSERINES and DOLLARBIRD

Passerines are the largest group of birds. They are small to medium sized land birds found worldwide, except on Antarctica. All species have four toes, three pointing forward and one back, well-adapted for perching. Most species are song-birds, with complex musical calls, but there are exceptions (e.g. crows). They show great diversity of form, behaviour and breeding biology.

BLACK-FACED CUCKOO-SHRIKE *Coracina novaehollandiae*
Rare Australian vagrant

33 cm. Large pale grey bird with a long tail, and *habit of folding and refolding its wings on alighting* at a perch. Adult has black face and throat. Immature has black patch from bill to ear coverts, and pale faintly barred throat and upper breast. Sexes alike. Flight undulating. Feeds mainly on insects taken in foliage or by swooping to the ground from a perch. Call a short soft croaky 'prurr'. **Habitat:** Lightly forested open country. Vagrants, mostly immatures, seen mainly in autumn, sometimes in spring.

DOLLARBIRD *Eurystomus orientalis*
Rare Australian straggler

29 cm. Stout short-tailed greenish bird with a large brownish head and glossy blue throat. Short broad red bill; red legs. In flight, *prominent pale 'silver dollar' patches on wings.* Immature has brown-grey body, dark bill and brown legs. Sexes alike. Perches high on dead branches, in an upright posture, before swooping out to catch large insects. Call a *loud raspy cackle.* **Habitat:** Lightly forested open country. Breeds Australia. Winters Asia. Most NZ records are of adults in Nov–Dec, and immatures in Mar–May.

SATIN FLYCATCHER *Myiagra cyanoleuca*
Rare Australian vagrant

16 cm. Small slim bird with a rather long tail; a small crest gives a *peaked back of head.* Male dark glossy *blue-black*, except lower chest and belly white. Female slate grey with bluish gloss on upperparts; throat and upperbreast reddish buff, *contrasts sharply* with white lower breast and belly. Feeds on insects by darting out from a perch to snatch them in mid-air. On realighting, quivers tail. **Habitat:** Of 3 NZ records, 2 seen in gardens.

WHITE-BROWED WOODSWALLOW *Artamus superciliosus*
Rare Australian vagrant

19 cm. In flight, like a small slim Starling soaring and gliding gracefully. Head, throat and upperparts dark blue-grey; chestnut underparts; a prominent broad white eyebrow in males, less distinct in females. Feeds on insects taken in the air and on the ground; also nectar. **Habitat:** Open country. Two NZ records.

MASKED WOODSWALLOW *Artamus personatus*
Rare Australian vagrant

19 cm. In flight, like a small slim Starling soaring and gliding gracefully. Males two-tone grey, darker above; *black face and throat mask*, bordered white. Females duller with less distinct mask. Feeds on insects taken in the air and on the ground; also nectar. **Habitat:** Open country. Only NZ record was a pair that bred in Otago in early 1970s.

WHITE-WINGED TRILLER *Lalage tricolor*
Rare Australian vagrant

18 cm. Breeding male black and white with a grey rump. Female and immature brown with buff feather edges. Non-breeding male like female, but wings black and white. Feeds mainly on insects taken in foliage or by swooping to ground from a perch. Male song, uttered while perched and in flight, is Chaffinch-like in form, a descending 'chiff-chiff-chiff-joey-joey-joey', ending with a Canary-like trill. **Habitat:** One NZ record: in a Dunedin garden, 1969.

BLACK-FACED CUCKOO-SHRIKE

imm

DOLLARBIRD

WHITE-BROWED
WOODSWALLOW

♀

♂

SATIN FLYCATCHER

♂

♀

♀

♂

♀

♂ breeding

MASKED WOODSWALLOW

WHITE-WINGED TRILLER

Plate 66

NATIVE PASSERINES

RIFLEMAN (Titipounamu) *Acanthisitta chloris* Locally common endemic

8 cm; ♂ 6 g, ♀ 7 g. *NZ's smallest bird. Rounded wings; very short stumpy tail;* bill fine and slightly upturned. Male bright yellow-green above, green on rump; female streaked dark and light brown above, brownish yellow on rump. Both whitish below, conspicuous white eyebrow stripe, and yellowish flanks. Immature like female but streaked on breast. Feeds by working its way up trees and shrubs, flicking wings and exploring bark and lichen of trunks, branches and leaves. Call a very high-pitched sharp repeated 'zipt', beyond the hearing range of some people. **Habitat:** Native forest and scrub; favours beech and tawa forest. Some in exotic forest, gorse and willows, especially in South I. **Breeding:** Sep–Feb.

ROCK WREN *Xenicus gilviventris* Uncommon endemic

10 cm; ♂ 16 g, ♀ 20 g. Small alpine bird with short tail, rounded wings, long legs and toes, fine black bill, cream eyebrow. Male dull green above, grey-brown below, flanks yellow; brighter green and yellow in Fiordland. Female plainer olive brown. *Bobs vigorously up and down.* Usually hops and runs, flying only short distances. **Habitat:** Alpine regions of South I only, among rockfalls, screes and subalpine scrub. **Breeding:** Oct–Feb.

SILVEREYE (Tauhou) *Zosterops lateralis* Abundant native

12 cm, 13 g. Small green bird with conspicuous *white eye-ring.* Head and upperparts olive green with grey back and wash on lower neck and onto breast; underparts creamy white with pinkish-brown flanks and white undertail. Sexes alike. Juvenile lacks eye-ring. Usually in small flocks, except when breeding. Readily attracted to bird tables in cold winters. Flight call from flocks an excited 'cli-cli-cli'; single birds give a plaintive 'cree'. Song a melodious mix of warbles, trills and slurs. **Habitat:** Forests, scrub, orchards, parks and gardens. **Breeding:** Sep–Mar.

GREY WARBLER (Riroriro) *Gerygone igata* Abundant endemic

10 cm, 6.5 g. Very small grey bird with a darker *tail, conspicuously tipped white,* and a habit of *hovering* to pick insects and spiders from plants. Adult is grey-brown above, pale grey on face, throat and breast; off-white belly and undertail, red eye. Sexes alike. Juvenile similar but yellowish on face and underparts, brown eye. Flits and hovers among outer foliage and twigs to catch invertebrates. Song a distinctive *long musical wavering trill.* **Habitat:** Scrub (especially manuka and kanuka), forest, parks and gardens. Builds a distinctive domed hanging nest, with small side entrance hole. **Breeding:** Aug–Jan.

CHATHAM ISLAND WARBLER *Gerygone albofrontata* Locally abundant endemic

12 cm; ♂ 10 g, ♀ 8.5 g. Like large Grey Warbler but browner and bill much larger. Male has olive-brown head and upperparts, darker on wings and tail; prominent *white forehead, eyebrow and underparts*; flanks and undertail pale yellow; red eye. Female lacks white forehead and has duller greyish-white underparts and yellowish eyebrow, face and throat. Juvenile like female, but upperparts olive grey; underparts yellower; eye brown. Gleans invertebrates from leaves and crevices in trunks and branches; rarely hovers. **Habitat:** Forest and scrub. Builds a distinctive domed hanging nest, with small side entrance hole. **Breeding:** Sep–Jan.

RIFLEMAN

♂

♀

ROCK WREN

♂

♀

SILVEREYE

juv

GREY WARBLER

CHATHAM ISLAND
WARBLER

♂

Plate 67

INTRODUCED PASSERINES and NEW ZEALAND PIPIT

BLACKBIRD *Turdus merula* **Abundant European introduction**

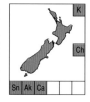

25 cm, 90 g. Adult male *black with a bright orange bill*. Adult female *dark brown* with paler throat and smudgy mottled breast; bill brown and dull orange. Juvenile *rusty brown*, especially on head; pale streaks on back and wing coverts; brown barring on underparts; bill dark brown. Immature male (Apr–Jan) has brown wings contrasting with black body. *Long tail*. Feeds mainly on the ground; *hops* rather than walks. *Song a loud clear tuneful warble, mellower than Song Thrush and not repetitive.* Alarm call a persistent sharp 'tchink-tchink'. **Habitat:** Forest, scrub, farmland with scattered trees or hedges, orchards, parks and gardens. **Breeding:** Aug–Jan.

SONG THRUSH *Turdus philomelos* **Abundant European introduction**

23 cm, 70 g. Warm brown above, buff-white below, with *breast boldly spotted dark brown*. Bill yellowish brown with yellow gape; legs pinkish brown. Sexes alike. Juvenile similar but more yellowish buff, spotted and streaked paler above and smaller spots below; bill dark brown with prominent yellow gape. Feeds mostly on the ground, where it hops and runs. Hammers snails open on a regular 'anvil'. Song *a loud string of repeated clear-cut musical phrases*, each separated by a brief pause: 'chitty-choo chitty-choo, oo-eee oo-eee . . .' Song perch usually high and conspicuous. **Habitat:** Forest, scrub, farmland with scattered trees or hedges, orchards, parks and gardens. **Breeding:** Aug–Feb.

Starling (juvenile — see Plate 73) **[Sp 319]**

DUNNOCK *Prunella modularis* **Common European introduction**

14 cm, 21 g. *Nondescript, dark and unobtrusive bird*, rather like a female House Sparrow but has *slim body, fine black bill*. Upperparts brown streaked darker; face, collar and breast washed grey; flanks streaked brown; red eye; orange-brown legs. Sexes alike. Juvenile similar but has brown eye. Usually feeds alone on the ground, keeping close to cover; shuffles along in a crouched posture, delicately picking at the surface. Sings from the top of a bush or hedge, a thin hurried warble. Call a high-pitched insistent 'tseep'. **Habitat:** Forest, scrub, farmland with hedges, orchards, parks and gardens. **Breeding:** Aug–Feb.

SKYLARK *Alauda arvensis* **Common European introduction**

18 cm, 38 g. Dull yellow-buff bird, streaked and spotted brown on upperparts and breast. Adult has a *small crest*, raised when alert. Juvenile yellower and spottier, and lacks crest. In flight, *white outer tail feathers and white trailing edge to broad wings*. Male in territorial flight display (Aug–Jan) soars with whirring wings up to 100 m, and slowly descends, all the time singing a *sustained and vigorous torrent of varied trills and runs*. Call, usually in flight, a liquid 'chirrup'. **Habitat:** Open country, from coast to subalpine. **Breeding:** Sep–Feb.

NEW ZEALAND PIPIT (Pihoihoi) *Anthus novaeseelandiae* **Uncommon native**

19 cm, 40 g. Like Skylark, including white outer tail feathers, but more slender and has the distinctive habit of frequently *flicking its long tail up and down*. Head and upperparts brown, streaked darker; prominent *white eyebrow*; underparts whitish, streaked brown on breast. Runs and walks jerkily on long legs; often flies a short distance ahead, calling a shrill 'scree' or drawn-out 'zwee'. **Habitat:** Open habitats from coast to alpine tops, but avoids intensively farmed areas; mainly near coast, on shingle riverbeds, gravel roads, and scree slopes. **Breeding:** Aug–Mar.

BLACKBIRD

♂

juv

♀

juv

SONG THRUSH

Starling juv

SKYLARK

DUNNOCK

NEW ZEALAND PIPIT

Plate 68

NATIVE PASSERINES

FERNBIRD (Matata) *Bowdleria punctata*   Locally common endemic

18 cm, 35 g. Warm brown above, paler below, heavily streaked and spotted dark brown; *forehead and crown chestnut*; whitish eyebrow stripe. Distinctive *long frayed tail*. Sexes and juveniles alike. Secretive, often remaining hidden in thick vegetation or moving mouse-like through the rushes, appearing inquisitively in the scrub canopy. Reluctant to fly. Flight weak and whirring, tail drooping. Often detected by sound alone. Common call a short sharp 'tchip', and *metallic double-note 'uu-tick'* often produced by pair in duet. **Habitat:** Freshwater and tidal wetlands, especially reedbeds or pakihi with emergent scrub; also drier sparse scrub and bracken. **Breeding:** Aug–Mar.

BROWN CREEPER (Pipipi) *Mohoua novaeseelandiae*   Locally common endemic

13 cm; ♂ 13.5 g, ♀ 11 g. Crown, back, rump and tail reddish brown; ash grey on face and neck; small white stripe behind eye; light buff underparts; dark bar near tip of tail. Sexes and juveniles alike. Usually in small fast-moving *noisy* flocks high in canopy, uttering nasal notes and rapid slurred trills. Male song includes slurs, musical whistles and harsh notes: 'chi-roh-ree-roh-ree-ree', the second note being lower than the first. Females sing a rapid sequence of brief notes, the last being higher and prolonged. **Habitat:** Forest and scrub of South and Stewart Is. **Breeding:** Sep–Feb.

WHITEHEAD (Popokatea) *Mohoua albicilla*   Locally common endemic

15 cm; ♂ 18.5 g, ♀ 14.5 g. Male has *white head and underparts*, with contrasting black bill, eye and legs; upperparts pale brown. Female and immature similar, but crown and nape shaded brown. Usually in small fast-moving *noisy* feeding flocks or family groups, high in canopy, uttering harsh chattering calls, trills and slurs. Male song can be clear and Canary-like: 'peek-o, peek-o, peek-o'. **Habitat:** Native and exotic forest, and scrub of North I. **Breeding:** Sep–Jan.

YELLOWHEAD (Mohua) *Mohoua ochrocephala*   Rare endemic

15 cm; ♂ 30 g, ♀ 25 g. Male has *bright yellow head and underparts* with contrasting black bill, eye and legs; upperparts yellowish brown. Female and immature similar, but crown and nape shaded brown. Tip of tail often worn to spine-like shafts. Usually in small *noisy* feeding flocks or family groups, high in canopy, uttering loud staccato chattering calls and trills and slurs. Male song clear and Canary-like. **Habitat:** Tall native forest, especially red beech of South I. **Breeding:** Oct–Feb.

FANTAIL (Piwakawaka) *Rhipidura fuliginosa*   Abundant native

16 cm (including 8 cm tail), 8 g. Small bird with small head and bill; *long tail, often fanned.* Pied phase has grey head, white eyebrow, brown back; yellow underparts, with white and black bands across chest; black and white tail. Juvenile similar, but browner body, rusty-brown wing coverts, and indistinct chest markings. Island subspecies have variable white in tail, most in Chathams. Black phase, mainly in South I, all sooty black except white spot behind eye. Restless movements; twists and jerks on a perch, tail fanned, flies out to seize flying insects. Erratic flight as it hawks over forest or scrub canopy, into an insect swarm over a clearing, paddock, pond or garden. Call a penetrating 'cheet'; song a harsh rhythmical 'saw-like' 'tweet-a-tweet-a-tweet-a-tweet . . .' **Habitat:** Forest, scrub, farmland with hedges and shelterbelts, river margins, parks and gardens. **Breeding:** Aug–Mar.

FERNBIRD

BROWN CREEPER

YELLOWHEAD

WHITEHEAD

pied phase

juv pied

FANTAIL

black phase

Plate 69

NATIVE PASSERINES

TOMTIT (Miromiro – North I, Ngiru-ngiru – South I) *Petroica macrocephala*
Common endemic

13 cm, 11 g. Small forest bird with a large head and short tail. Five subspecies vary slightly in size and colour; the most distinctive is the Snares subspecies, which is wholly black but glossier in the male. Adult male (North I) has black head with small white spot above bill; glossy black upperparts and upper breast; white underparts, sharply divided at breast; white wingbar and sides to tail. South, Chatham and Auckland Is subspecies similar, but have underparts yellowish, brighter or orange on upper breast near dividing line. Juvenile males similar, but have white shaft streaks to black feathers and always have white underparts. Adult females (North and South Is) have brown head and upperparts; grey-brown chin and upper breast fading to white on underparts; wingbar and sides of tail pale buff. Chatham I female similar but darker brown above. Auckland Is female like male but dull black upperparts and upper breast. Feeds in the understorey by perching on branch or trunk, scanning, then flying to ground or tree to catch invertebrates. *Male song a loud jingling burst: 'ti oly oly oly oh'*, varies regionally. Male call a short high-pitched 'swee'; female call a reedy 'seet'. **Habitat:** Scrub, native and exotic forest and scrub. **Breeding:** Sep–Feb.

BLACK ROBIN *Petroica traversi*
Rare endemic

15 cm; ♂ 25 g, ♀ 22 g. Small completely black forest bird with short fine black bill, long thin legs and an upright stance. Feeds mostly on the forest floor or in low branches. Male song a clear simple phrase of 5–7 notes. Call a high-pitched single note. Formerly extremely rare; in 1979 there were just 5 birds, including 1 productive female 'Old Blue' (depicted), but with intensive management the population has recovered to about 150. **Habitat:** Forest and scrub of predator-free islands in Chathams group. **Breeding:** Oct–Jan.

NEW ZEALAND ROBIN (Toutouwai) *Petroica australis*
Uncommon endemic

18 cm, 35 g. Inquisitive and confiding *dark slaty-grey forest bird with long thin legs and an upright stance.* Male (North I) is dark, almost black, except for white spot above bill, pale greyish-white lower breast and belly; black feathers have pale shaft streaks, and so very faintly streaked upperparts; wings dark brownish black. Female and juvenile (North I) similar, but greyer with variable paler patches on breast and throat. Male (South I) has dark grey upperparts and upper chest, distinctly divided from yellowish-white lower chest and belly; flanks variably greyish; white spot above bill; wings dark brownish black. Female and juvenile (South I) similar, usually greyer on breast with variable whitish patches. Stewart I birds have similar patterns to North I. Perches on a low trunk or branch and flies to *feed on the forest floor*; hops about and sometimes trembles one leg to induce prey to surface. Male song loud clear and sustained string of phrases, usually descending and including 'pwee-pwee-pwee' phrases; varies regionally. Call a soft 'chirp'. **Habitat:** Native and exotic forest, sometimes tall scrub. **Breeding:** Jul–Jan.

TOMTIT

North Island ♂

♀

South Island

juv ♂

♂

Snares Island

BLACK ROBIN

North Island ♀

South Island ♂

♀

♂

juv

NEW ZEALAND ROBIN

Plate 70

NATIVE PASSERINES

KOKAKO   *Callaeas cinerea*   **Rare endemic**

38 cm, 230 g. *Large dark bluish-grey* bird with a *black facial mask*, short strongly arched black bill, long black legs, long tail and rounded wings. North I adult has blue wattles; South I adult has orange wattles. Juvenile has smaller pinkish wattles, smaller facial mask, and dull brown wash in plumage. Leaps around in trees and takes short flights, never sustained for long. More often heard than seen. Calls mostly at dawn; *song is a slow string of very loud rich mournful organ-like notes.* **Habitat:** Mainly tall podocarp hardwood forest in North I, Little Barrier, Tiritiri Matangi and Kapiti Is; formerly beech and mixed forest in South and Stewart Is, probably extinct. **Breeding:** Oct–Mar.

TUI   *Prosthemadera novaeseelandiae*   **Common endemic**

30 cm; ♂ 120 g, ♀ 90 g. Dark bird with two *white throat tufts*, or poi. Looks black in dull light, but has *green, bluish-purple and bronze iridescent sheen*, back and flanks dark reddish brown; a lacy collar of filamentous white feathers on neck; white wingbar; slightly decurved black bill and strong black legs. Sexes alike. Juvenile dull slate black with glossy wings and tail, greyish-white throat, lacks tufts. Energetic and acrobatic while feeding in trees on nectar and fruit. In flight, round wings with white shoulder patches; long broad tail; *noisy whirring flight* between short glides. Song has rich fluid melodic notes (often repeated) mixed with coughs, clicks, grunts and wheezes; varies regionally. **Habitat:** Native forest and scrub, farmland with kowhai, gums and flax, parks and gardens. **Breeding:** Sep–Feb.

STITCHBIRD (Hihi)   *Notiomystis cincta*   **Rare endemic**

18 cm; ♂ 40 g, ♀ 30 g. Male has white erectile tufts behind eyes; velvety black head, upper breast and back, bordered golden yellow across breast and folded wings; rest of underparts pale brown. Female greyish brown with white wingbar; lacks ear tufts. Often cocks tail. Call an loud explosive whistle: 'see-si-ip'. **Habitat:** Forest on a few predator-free islands, especially Little Barrier, Tiritiri Matangi, Kapiti and Mokoia. **Breeding:** Sep–Apr.

BELLBIRD (Korimako, Makomako)   *Anthornis melanura*   **Common endemic**

20 cm; ♂ 34 g, ♀ 26 g. Green bird with a short curved bill, slightly forked tail, and noisy whirring fast and direct flight. Adult male olive green, paler on underparts, head tinted with purple gloss; wings and tail dark bluish black, except for yellow patch at bend of folded wing; eye red. Female browner with *narrow white stripe across cheek from bill* and bluish gloss on forehead and crown. Juvenile like female, but with *brown eye and yellowish cheek stripe.* Song varies regionally but always loud clear liquid ringing notes, without grunts and wheezes. Alarm call a rapidly repeated harsh scolding 'yeng, yeng, yeng'. **Habitat:** Native and exotic forest, scrub, farm shelter-belts, parks and gardens. **Breeding:** Sep–Feb.

SADDLEBACK (Tieke)   *Philesturnus carunculatus*   **Rare endemic**

25 cm; ♂ 80 g, ♀ 70 g. Head and body glossy black with *bright chestnut saddle*, rump and tail coverts; *pendulous orange-red wattles at base of black bill.* North I subspecies has thin buff line at upper edge of saddle. North I juvenile has smaller wattles and lacks buff line; South I juvenile (Jackbird) *chocolate brown*, paler below, with reddish-brown tail coverts, and small wattles. Often feeds on the forest floor, and bounds from branch to branch rather than flies. Main call is a *strident ringing 'cheet, te-te-te-te'*; often duet. **Habitat:** Forest and scrub on several offshore islands. **Breeding:** Aug–May.

KOKAKO

North Island

juv

South Island

TUI

juv

STITCHBIRD

♂

♀

juv ♂

BELLBIRD

SADDLEBACK

juv South Island

♂

ad North Island

♀

Plate 71

INTRODUCED PASSERINES

HOUSE SPARROW   *Passer domesticus*   Abundant European introduction

14 cm, 30 g. A gregarious, garrulous and quarrelsome associate of humans. Conical bill. Adult male chestnut brown above, streaked black on back; crown *dark grey*; rump greyish brown; underparts greyish white. Black bib and bill in breeding season, bib smaller and bill greyish pink rest of year. Female and juvenile drab sandy brown above, streaked darker on back; greyish white below; pale buffy eyebrow and sides to neck. Young juvenile often shows fleshy yellow gape. Flight fast and direct, showing small white wingbar. Voice a variety of monotonous unmusical cheeps and chirps. **Habitat:** Towns, arable farmland and farm shelterbelts, orchards; sometimes edges of native forest well away from human habitation. **Breeding:** Sep–Feb.

CHAFFINCH   *Fringilla coelebs*   Abundant European introduction

15 cm; ♂ 22 g, ♀ 21 g. Sparrow-sized finch with *conspicuous white shoulder, wingbar and outer tail feathers*. Adult male has black forehead, blue-grey crown and nape; *rich pinkish-brown face and underparts*, fading to white on belly; reddish-brown back; olive rump. Female and juvenile lack male colours; mainly soft brownish grey, except greenish rump and prominent white wingbars on darker wing. Flight undulating; flight call a soft single 'tsip'. *Male song a series of short loud notes, ending in a flourish:* *'chip chip chip tell tell tell cherry-erry-erry tissi cheweeo'*, usually given from a high perch. Usual calls a metallic 'pink' or 'chwink-chwink', and a whistling 'huit'. **Habitat:** Native and exotic forest, scrub, farmland, tussockland, parks and gardens. **Breeding:** Sep–Feb.

REDPOLL   *Carduelis flammea*   Common European introduction

12 cm, 12 g. Small dull brown-streaked finch, but seen closely *forehead crimson and chin black*. Male in breeding season develops a pink to crimson flush on its breast, varying in intensity with individual and region. Juvenile lacks the crimson and black on the head and can look pale-headed. Often seen feeding or flying in large flocks, especially near weed-infested crops. Flight erratic and undulating; *flight call a fast harsh rattling metallic 'chich-chich-chich'*, sometimes followed by a 'bizzzz'. Main call a plaintive, questioning 'tsooeet?'. **Habitat:** Farmland, orchards, tussockland, forest and scrub margins, parks and gardens. **Breeding:** Oct–Feb.

GOLDFINCH   *Carduelis carduelis*   Abundant European introduction

13 cm; ♂ 16 g, ♀ 15 g. Small finch with *striking gold bars on black wings*. Adults have *brilliant red face*, slightly more extensive on the male, especially above and behind the eye; white ear coverts and sides to neck; black crown and half-collar; upperparts and breast soft brown; rest of underparts and rump white; tail black, spotted white near tip. Juvenile pale buff, streaked and spotted darker; wings and tail as in adult. Outside breeding season, usually in flocks, often feeding on seeds of thistles or other weeds. Flight undulating. *Male song a pleasant liquid twittering 'tsitt-witt-witt'*. **Habitat:** Farmland, orchards, parks and gardens. **Breeding:** Oct–Mar.

♂ breeding
♂ non-breeding
♀

HOUSE SPARROW

♀
♂

CHAFFINCH

♀
juv
REDPOLL
♂ breeding

juv
GOLDFINCH

Plate 72

INTRODUCED PASSERINES

GREENFINCH   *Carduelis chloris*   Common European introduction

15 cm, 28 g. *A robust olive-green finch with a pale heavy bill and prominent yellow on the sides of the tail and the edges of the closed wing.* Males olive green, the brightest have a conspicuous yellow eyebrow and yellowish belly. Females browner, dull olive green, the dullest a washed-out greenish brown. Juvenile and many immatures duller again, mainly brown, streaked darker with yellowish-green wash on rump and upper tail coverts. Flight undulating, looking heavy-bodied and short-tailed, and showing yellow wing flashes. Out of breeding season, often form large flocks in weed-infested crops. In breeding season, male repeatedly calls a *harsh drawn-out 'dzwee'*. Other common calls are a pleasant twittering 'chichichichichit-teu-teu-teu-teu', sometimes just the 'teu' notes; and a sweet rising 'tsooeet'. **Habitat:** Farmland, pine plantations, native bush and scrub fringes, pine and macrocarpa shelterbelts, parks and gardens. **Breeding:** Oct–Mar.

YELLOWHAMMER   *Emberiza citrinella*   Common European introduction

16 cm, 27 g. Sparrow-sized mainly *yellow bird of open country* with reddish-brown upperparts, streaked darker; *rufous rump and white outer tail feathers.* Adult male has *bright yellow head and underparts,* head lightly marked brown on crown and on sides of face; *cinnamon wash across breast,* and pale yellow flanks. Adult female duller and paler yellow, more heavily marked brown on head, and *breast band greyish green.* Juvenile and immature even paler yellow or pale buff, heavily streaked, but still with rufous rump. Hops on ground when feeding, often with crouched posture. Outside breeding season, often form flocks on weed-infested crops and where hay has been scattered. Male song is rendered 'little bit of bread and no cheese'. Call a ringing metallic 'tink', or 'twick'. **Habitat:** Open country from sea level to sub-alpine, especially arable farmland or rough pasture with scattered scrub. **Breeding:** Oct–Mar.

CIRL BUNTING   *Emberiza cirlus*   Uncommon European introduction

16 cm, 25 g. Sparrow-sized bird of open country, similar to Yellowhammer in size and shape and also with white outer tail feathers, but much less yellow and *rump greyish olive.* Adult male distinctive with black throat, head boldly striped black and yellow, crown and nape dark grey, fading to pale grey wash across breast; upperparts brown, streaked darker; cinnamon patches on wings and sides of lower breast, rest of underparts pale yellow streaked darker. Adult female and juvenile nondescript mix of buff, yellow and brown, heavily streaked on crown and finely streaked on breast and flanks. Hops on ground when feeding, often with crouched posture. Outside breeding season, often form small flocks on waste ground. Male song a *monotonous metallic cricket-like rattling buzz.* Calls include a thin 'zit' or 'see', and a soft brief 'tyu'. **Habitat:** Dry pastoral or arable farmland with scattered scrub, and pine and macrocarpa shelterbelts, mainly in Nelson and eastern South I, especially Marlborough and Central Otago. Some move to coastal wasteland and saltmarsh in winter. **Breeding:** Oct–Feb.

House Sparrow (female — see Plate 71)

GREENFINCH

♀

♂

juv

YELLOWHAMMER

♀

♂

juv

CIRL BUNTING

♀

juv

♂

♀ House Sparrow

Plate 73

INTRODUCED PASSERINES

STARLING *Sturnus vulgaris*   **Abundant European introduction**

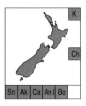

21 cm, 85 g. *Short-tailed dark bird with waddling jerky walk.* Breeding adult glossy black with purple sheen on head and breast; dark green sheen and buff spangling on wings and abdomen; pointed yellow bill, bluish base in male, pinkish in female. Non-breeding head and body spotted buff and white; bill dark. Juvenile smooth grey-brown, throat paler; bill dark. Flight fast and direct, often in large co-ordinated flocks. Distinctly *pointed triangular wings*. Large winter roosts; flocks converge at dusk and disperse at dawn. Feeds on ground by jabbing bill into soil. *Noisy*; call a descending whistle: 'cheeoo'; song, a rambling collection of clicks, rattles, warbles and gargles, interspersed with musical whistles. A good mimic. **Habitat:** Farmland, orchards, parks, gardens, city streets, forest margins and beaches. **Breeding:** Oct–Jan.

RED-VENTED BULBUL *Pycnonotus cafer*   **Rare Asian introduction**

20 cm. Slim dark bird with long *white-tipped tail and red patch on undertail.* Head, upperparts and breast blackish, fading to grey on belly; rump white. Feathers on back of head can be raised into triangular crest. A popular cage-bird because of cheerful attractive call: 'pee pee-plo' or 'be-care-ful'. **Habitat:** Parks and gardens of central Auckland; established in 1950s, then exterminated, but others have been illegally released in 1990s.

MYNA *Acridotheres tristis*   **Locally abundant Asian introduction**

24 cm, 125 g. *Cheeky brown bird with jaunty walk.* Adult *cinnamon brown with glossy black head and neck*, white undertail and underwing; yellow legs, bill and bare patch of skin near eye. Sexes alike. Juvenile has dark brown head, paler bill and facial skin. In flight, prominent *white patches on wings*, and white-tipped tail. Roosts communally all year, largest in winter; small flocks converge at dusk and depart at dawn. Feeds mainly on the ground, *often at roadsides*. Voice jangling; song a rapid medley of raucous gurgling, chattering and bell-like notes. **Habitat:** Parks, gardens, orchards and farmland, sometimes on forest margins. **Breeding:** Oct–Mar.

AUSTRALIAN MAGPIE *Gymnorhina tibicen*   **Abundant Australian introduction**

41 cm, 350 g. Large *black and white bird with pale blue black-tipped bill.* White-backed form has *hind neck and back white* in male, *finely barred grey* in female. Black-backed form (mostly in Hawke's Bay), has *black back*; hind neck white in male, finely barred grey in female. Juvenile like female, but underparts brownish grey and bill dark. Hybrids have variable black on back. Flight direct, with pointed wings and rapid shallow wingbeats. Feeds on the ground, sometimes in loose flocks. Song distinctive flute-like carolling, especially at dawn and dusk, rendered 'quardle oodle ardle wardle doodle'. **Habitat:** Open farmland with tall shelterbelts and scattered trees or forest, parks and gardens. **Breeding:** Jul–Dec.

ROOK *Corvus frugilegus*   **Locally common European introduction**

45 cm; ♂ 425 g, ♀ 375 g. A *large glossy black crow with shaggy feathered thighs.* Adult has bare whitish face. Juvenile and immature have faces feathered black. In flight, *long broad 'fingered' wings*, broad roundish tail. *Flight strong and direct, but languid.* Feeds mainly on ground; walks sedately with occasional hops. Feeds, roosts and nests in flocks. Often wary and give *coarse 'caw' or 'kaah' calls* if disturbed or in flight. **Habitat:** Pasture and cultivated paddocks, farm shelterbelts, especially tall gums and pines. **Breeding:** Aug–Dec.

juv

breeding

non-breeding

STARLING

RED-VENTED
BULBUL

MYNA

juv

juv
white-backed

♀

white-backed

AUSTRALIAN
MAGPIE

ROOK

imm

ack-backed

♂

Plate 74

SPECIES EXTINCT SINCE 1900

New Zealand, like many other isolated island groups, has a long history of bird extinction. About 32 species died out in the 800 years between the arrival of Polynesians and the arrival of Europeans, most notably all the moa species. In the 200 years since European contact, 9 further species have become extinct, 5 of which have probably died out since 1900. The main factors that contributed to extinction were loss of habitat, introduced mammalian predators and overharvesting.

PIOPIO *Turnagra capensis*   Probably extinct endemic

26 cm. Plump olive-brown Blackbird-sized forest bird. Upperparts olive brown; upper tail coverts and tail rust red, except olive-brown central tail feathers; short robust dark brown bill; legs dark brown. North I subspecies had *white throat*; olive-grey breast and belly, the under tail coverts washed yellow. South I subspecies was *boldly streaked brown and white below*, throat and sides of neck tinged reddish brown, and feathers of forehead, crown and face tipped rust red. Song varied and sustained with 5 distinct bars, each repeated 6–7 times. Common call a short, sharp, whistling cry, quickly repeated. **Habitat:** Native forest and scrub; last confirmed record King Country, 1902, but more recent reports from inland Taranaki, Urewera, western Nelson and Fiordland.

LAUGHING OWL (Whekau) *Sceloglaux albifacies*   Extinct endemic

38 cm. A large owl with *yellowish-brown plumage heavily streaked brown. Face white around dark reddish-brown eye*, chin greyish; white splashes on scapulars, sometimes also on hindneck and mantle; wings and tail brown with brownish-white bars; bill horn-coloured, black at base; long well-feathered yellowish to reddish-buff legs. Calls, mainly on dark nights, 'a loud cry made up of a series of dismal shrieks frequently repeated', and 'a peculiar barking noise'. **Habitat:** Forests, scrub and open country with rock and limestone outcrops for cover. Last recorded South Canterbury, 1914.

HUIA *Heteralocha acutirostris*   Extinct endemic

♂ 45 cm, ♀ 48 cm. Glossy black with bluish iridescence, last 3 cm of long tail white; rounded orange wattles at base of ivory-white bill with greyish base: *male had stout straight 60 mm bill, female had slender curved 105 mm bill*; legs bluish grey. Immature had duller plumage, white tip of tail tinged reddish buff, wattles small and pale. Call a soft clear whistle; also a whistling note of higher pitch. **Habitat:** Native forest of southern North I since 1840. Last accepted record 1907.

BUSH WREN *Xenicus longipes*   Probably extinct endemic

9 cm, 16 g. Larger and darker than Rifleman but easily missed in the gloom of the forest. *Head dark olive brown with clear white eyebrow-stripe*; upperparts dark yellowish green, dark green tail; chin greyish white, *ash-grey underparts* except yellow flanks; long feet and toes. Female and Stewart I subspecies browner. Like the Rock Wren, *bobs on alighting on the ground.* **Habitat:** Forest and scrub. Last records: Urewera, 1955; Nelson Lakes NP, 1968; Kaimohu I (off Stewart I), 1972.   **[Sp 284]**

AUCKLAND ISLAND MERGANSER *Mergus australis*   Extinct endemic

58 cm. Distinctive slim shag-like bird. *Dark red-brown head* with long feathers on back of head forming a wispy crest; upperparts dark greyish brown; underparts grey with white mottling. *Long slender orange-yellow bill*, browner above and serrated along cutting edges; legs orange. In flight, white wing-patch and underwing white mottled grey. Sexes alike. **Habitat:** Restricted to coastal waters and streams of Auckland Is since European settlement. Last recorded 1902.

PIOPIO

North Island

South Island

LAUGHING OWL

HUIA

♂

♀

BUSH WREN

♂

♀

AUCKLAND ISLAND
MERGANSER

INDEX

INDEX